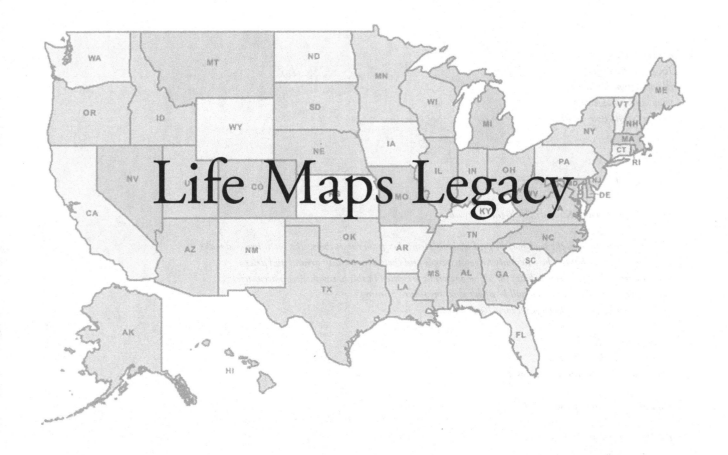

Life Maps Legacy

Kennedy and Kennedy

authorHOUSE®

AuthorHouse™
1663 Liberty Drive
Bloomington, IN 47403
www.authorhouse.com
Phone: 1-800-839-8640

A Life Map Legacy Series

Editor: Cillon McKenley
Cover design: Margret Dixon
Illustrator: Barbara Thomas Campbell

Published by AuthorHouse 12/20/2012

ISBN: 978-1-4772-9372-0 (sc)
*   978-1-4772-9373-7 (e)*

Library of Congress Control Number: 2012915351

DEDICATION

This book is dedicated to our six grand children – Jehylessa, Brittni, Robert IV, Leighvanni, Jayden and Darius – who are just beginning their exploration of the world, and who we trust, will find the way to a successful destiny. It is our hope that, as the principles outlined in the manual have been impacting our children and grand-children, in turn they might also impact many with whom they are shared for shared.

Life begins with a playful dream
and ends with a stalk of reality.

Endorsements

Delightful Destiny or Dead End: Life Map Legacy is a pinpointed, thought provoking, practical, relevant and necessary workbook for adults, but especially teens and youths. Drs. Robert and June Kennedy, practitioners in the field of counseling individuals and groups, have mastered the art of communicating their message through writing. In an age of societal regression, low self-esteem, rising juvenile delinquency, teen peer pressure, drug and alcohol abuse, and eroding family values, this workbook comes as an oasis for the post-modern generation. The authors challenge youngsters to think, reflect, plan, dream, start over, control, organize and conceptualize life in a challenging frame. Their style of writing is engaging. Their illustrations, some drawn from sports icons, powerful, and their knowledge base and expertise make this workbook an excellent treasure. Life in the 21st Century has become more daunting for youths. *"Delightful Destiny or Dead End!"* is a resource material that helps to make the life of youths more simple to live. I say kudos for a work well done.

Alanzo H. Smith, D. Min., Ed. D. Director: Family Ministries, Greater NY Conference of SDA, Licensed Marriage & Family Therapist, Licensed Mental Health Counselor.

The material presented in this manual is exciting and inspirational. It is a most effective tool for those who desire to help young people gain direction on their life's pathway. It represents the quintessence of what every educator needs to help young people find their way during the turbulent period of life called "adolescence". The contents should be incorporated in the curriculum of our Christian Schools. It can provide our young people with relevant tools for negotiating a successful life. While it is important to help parents understand their adolescents, it is also crucial that we help our young people find their pathway to success. This material by the Kennedys is right on target and families, schools, churches and the society at large can benefit from the insights provided.

Nephtaly Dorzilme, D. Min., Pastor, Ontario Conference of SDA, Ontario, Canada

The life one leads is not only a path to one's own success, but a path for others. In this work the Kennedys have truly carved a path to success. They have given powerful guidance to anyone who wishes to stay away from distractions and detours, not only on their earthly historical journey, but they have shown the way to a spiritual destiny, through Life Map Legacy.

Stanley Bowen, CEO Antigua and Barbuda Christian Media Network.

Is your family "empowered" or "in peril?" If you're looking for relevant, current and spiritual answers to the challenging issues that are plaguing our youths, then you've found them! *Delightful Destiny or Dead End* is an invaluable resource for parents, educators, and therapist. This manual not only gets our heads out of the sand, it clears our eyes and gives us direction where and how we can lead our youth. Drs. D. Robert and S. June Kennedy's book is a defining work—a catalyst for any mentor seeking to touch young people's lives.

John A. Trusty, D.Min., LMFT, Relationship Director, Allegheny East Conference of Seventh-day Adventist, Pine Forge, Pennsylvania.

This manual is definitely among one of the most exhilarating I have encountered in my effort to bring direction to young people. It gives a step by step description on how one can succeed in life. Although it is intended for young people, it can also benefit a wide range of individuals in decision-making processes. It might also be used as a coaching tool for many different settings.

Reverend Emmanes Doxy, D.D, Pastor, The Great Commission Ministry Church, Newark, NJ

This is a unique motivational manual that challenges the myths and negative stereotypical ideas that are focused on parents and youths. These 14 dynamic steps towards success are compelling. They blend spiritual, emotional, philosophical, sociological, physical, and historical ideas together, showing carefully structured vision. The Kennedys' expertise in religion and education has allowed them to provide this document as a healing voice to current societal problems. The authors have strategically helped to develop critical thinking, and have provided real life examples as servant leaders.

Use the book. It will provide clues to bridge the gap between your dreams and reality by:

- Drawing on your inner creativity

- Developing your self-leadership/self-esteem

- Helping you to set goals

- Leading you to take courageous risk

- Assisting you to provide leadership for others

- Giving you a mountaintop experience

Life Maps Legacy will contribute to the debate on the problems of young people and provide hope towards a *Delightful Destiny*. Many years of work have created an excellent, provocative, practical, resourceful, selfless, and motivational work that only wise persons of great experience could produce. Very well done!

Sonia J. Rodney-Williams, Ed. D.: Department of Education, NYC.

> *The games we play can create a regulated map of our personality and potentiality. It is therefore of interest that this work is based on a game of life.*

CONTENTS

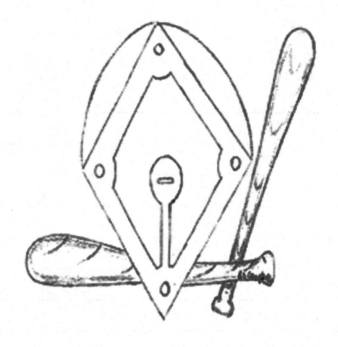

Filling each moment of your life
is what makes you who you are.

Introduction

It is a troubling reality to us that a great number of youngsters and parents that we have encountered have no sense of direction, and finds it difficult to make positive decisions in order to script a successful destination. Many seem to have no sense of who they are, where they want to go with their lives, or how to get there. They give the impression of being totally in charge, but in essence, they are confused. They are off to somewhere, "to another world" perhaps, but not a world of reality where they can feel the delights of a successful life.

Life Maps Legacy series are offered to help youngsters, as well as adults, gain a focus on how to use a strategic plan of action for the successful achievement of their life's destiny. It purports that destiny is a choice, and that to secure a positive destiny, one needs to follow a map of at least fourteen dynamic steps. Without a map, one can expect all kinds of distractions and dysfunctions, which will ultimately lead to destruction.

The Life Maps Legacy series are focused primarily on youngsters, but are also customer friendly for parents who seek to guide their adolescents or young adults who are seeking to build a life of success. In seven sessions the participants are led through fourteen steps to clarify their destination, establish positive direction and make critical decisions so that they will ultimately be delighted with their accomplishments.

How does a person transform inevitable failures into successes? What does one do when one feels trapped in a particular life situation? One might choose to spend the rest of his/her life blaming others, or one can learn how to get up and go, not discounting the help of others. It is foolish people who try to do everything on their own. An individual might write a note talking about negative history or might find constructive energy for effective execution. We have heard people whining about the poor circumstances of their birth, while talk about the impact of discrimination on their family. Others speak of the school systems in which they were educated, or the negative structures of their families. All these, and other negative realities are to be acknowledged, for they do impact people's opportunities for success. However, if people will learn that negative energy can be transformed into positive actions, there will be success where many possibilities of failure now reside.

Even when life does not always seem to produce success at every stage, there are always profound lessons to learn from failure and how to achieve a successful end game. The reality is that true success is not chance or a fleeting fame but that which has a realized dream. Baseball players know that with all things being equal, seventy percent failure and thirty percent success can bring their dreams to the Hall of Fame. The baseball "pit" is language mostly relevant to pitchers. However, it has significance for all players who understand that sacrifice, sweat and suffering are what will help one to win a game. One cannot stay in the "pit" to win. The "pit" is only the place for practice. The pit is the place where the foundations for success begin. It represents the place of struggle, but also the place where one sees opportunities for success. For example, if one pitch does not work, a pitcher can return to the pit and learn another. We see in the "pit" a spiritual connection with the biblical story of Joseph (Genesis 37, 39-50), whose dreams took him to a pit, but when he came from "the pit" he became the chief in Potiphar's house and later one of the most distinguished governors of Egypt. We have seen people who have lived with despair in the pit, but we have also see that one who succeed has found a way to climb out of their pits. Take special note of the comment in the box.

The Real Tragedy of Life

It must be borne in mind that the tragedy of
life doesn't lie in not reaching your goal.
The tragedy lies in having no goal to reach.

It is not a calamity to die with
dreams unfulfilled.
But it is a calamity not to dream.

It is not a disaster to be unable to
capture your ideal,
But it is a disaster to have no
ideal to capture.

It is not a disgrace not to reach the stars.
But it is a disgrace not to have stars
to reach for.

Not failure, but low aim is a sin.
Dr. Benjamin Elijah Mays

DREAMING

PERSPECTIVES ON YOUR LIFE

The road of life is filled with dreamers; some whose dreams are grounded in reality, bounded by authenticity and directed to triumph. There are others who are daydreamers, hallucinaters, whose dreams have become nightmares - **broken dreams.** While, for example, Dr. Martin Luther King Jr said he saw an American Dream, Malcolm X said he saw an American Nightmare. The question for everyone is whether we will live our lives out of a dream or out of a nightmare?

Yes, every person who walks the road of life needs a dream, and not only a dream, but how to keep that dream from becoming a nightmare. Some individuals are always looking for the pot of gold at the end of the rainbow. Some have become the slaves of the advertisement that says, "The real pot of gold at the end of the rainbow is Beer." Of course, it is of interest because anyone who is looking for gold at the end of the rainbow is living a dream and he is doomed to fail. Those Richard Rogers and Hammerstein used in the *Sound of Music* are profoundly encouraging in many ways; they grasped our attention, but in reality are flawed in some ways, when they said:

Climb every mountain,
Search high and low,
Follow every highway,
Every path you know.

Climb every mountain,
Ford every stream,
Follow every rainbow,
'Till you find your dream.

A dream that will need
All the love you can give,
Every day of your life
For as long as you live.

A successful destiny involves more than a dream, but dreaming is important. A dream that is rooted in reality gives us something to hope for and something to achieve. Henry Thoreau says that one needs to move confidently in the direction of one's dreams until the dream is achieved.

Dreaming and Road Maps

By way of a classic description, a dream is a road map, a mental map, a succession of images, ideas, emotions, and sensations that occur in the mind in certain stages of sleep or awareness. These images, ideas, emotions, and sensations have their foundation in the subconscious but are brought to the conscious because of the dream. When through the dream they make strong impact on the mind they become transformational, that is, they can change the personality and the direction of life.

We are not interpreters of dreams, and do not pretend to understand the psychology of dreams. In fact, it is our opinion that there is a demonic side to dreaming. By this we mean that the devil can use dreams to manipulate the minds of human beings into terrors of the night. But it is also apparent that there are wonderful dreamers and dreams that are under the control of a positive spiritual force that blesses human lives and guides their paths to triumph. Dream interpreters say that:

1. Dreams have an incubation period – a time when the dream stays in the subconscious and the images, ideas, emotions, and sensations are expanded until they come to the conscious as reality. Whether the images, ideas, etc., are false or true they take over the mind and control it for however long it will be allowed.

2. Dreams have an activation period – that is, the time when they move beyond the incubation and burst out of the egg. At such a stage they can be nurtured to grow or they can be left alone and waste away.

3. Dreams have a nurturing period – that is, the time what dreams are made to grow. We seek to find the meaning in the dreams and if we like the meaning we nurture them and let them help us find the way to the future. If he or she feels one has achieved a part of a dream then dream again to keep the dream expanding. One of the reasons we like baseball is that baseball is "A game of dreams." We have learned that one cannot just dream of it, one has to play it, but he or she must dream success constantly and maintain the momentum. It starts at home base but one has to go around the bases to develop the dream. It requires profound dedication and determination to follow the dream.

4. Dreams have a realization period - When we dream our destiny we have to learn how to create the bridge between our dream and reality. When reality is reached one needs to dream again. By constantly dreaming, the dreamer is able to fulfill not only their goal but attain a successful life.

Martin Luther King Jr. had much to say about "The Power of a Dream," not only in his "I have a dream" speech, but he was able to accomplish all that he did because he built his life on a dream.

Harriet Tubman, the civil rights activist who lived from 1820-1913 said, "Every great dream begins with a dreamer ... you have within you the strength, the patience, and the passion to reach for the stars to change the world."

Here is a visual diagram of what might be in your dream

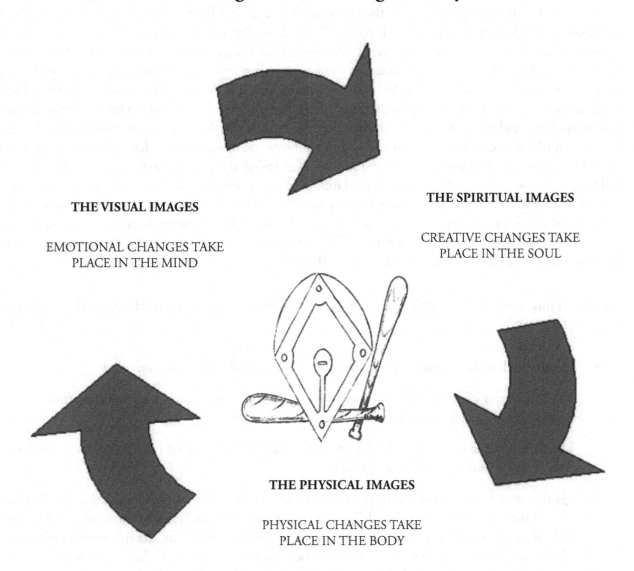

THE VISUAL IMAGES

EMOTIONAL CHANGES TAKE
PLACE IN THE MIND

THE SPIRITUAL IMAGES

CREATIVE CHANGES TAKE
PLACE IN THE SOUL

THE PHYSICAL IMAGES

PHYSICAL CHANGES TAKE
PLACE IN THE BODY

When a baseball season is over and players' dreams are dashed by personal or team failure, injuries, unrealized potential, and distractions, the players will return for another season, but they must go home and keep dreaming. Even if a player has been very successful in a season, his past successes cannot be used to determine future accomplishments. One has to celebrate each moment or period of success and dream again. What is true of baseball and dreaming is true of every game and is true of life. One has to celebrate one's dreams and keep nurturing it.

HOW GOD CAN DIRECT A LIFE THROUGH DREAMS

One of the most fascinating historical characters that we like to talk about is a Bible character called Jacob. His story is of interest because he fits into the mold of many in the game of life; who become confused on the road to success and think they can push their way to the top, by lying and cheating. The preface of Jacob's life is that he schemed and stole his brother, Esau's, birth-right, thus making Esau so angry that he plotted to kill Jacob. Upon hearing of the plot, their mother, Rebecca, decided to avoid murder in the family, and sent Jacob in quick flight to their uncle Laban in Padan Aran. During his flight Jacob had a dream. He had come to a place in the open field where he decided to stay for a night, because the sun had set. He took one of the stones of the place and put it under his head for a pillow and lay down to sleep. In the midst of the night, he dreamed that there was a ladder set up on the earth, and the top of it reached to heaven. He saw angels of God ascending and descending on the ladder. Then he noticed the Lord standing above the ladder and beside him. And the Lord said, "I am the Lord, the God of Abraham your father and the God of Isaac; the land on which you lie I will give to you and to your descendants; and your descendants shall be like the dust of the earth, and you shall spread abroad to the west and to the east and to the north and to the south; and by you and your descendants shall all the families of the earth bless themselves. Behold, I am with you and will keep you wherever you go, and will bring you back to this land; for I will not leave you until I have done that of which I have spoken to you." After the Lord spoke, Jacob awoke from his sleep and said, "Surely the Lord is in this place; and I did not know it." He then became afraid, and said, "This is none other than the house of God, and this is the gate of heaven." (For the complete story see Genesis 27, 28)

The dream might seem quite simple and we might extract many lessons from it. However, the simple points we extract are that:

- The dream led Jacob to see that he was not in charge of his life. God was.

- The dream was given to help fix Jacob's life. It allowed him to enter into a process that would lead to his repentance for what he had done to his brother.

- The dream challenged Jacob to a larger vision than he had scripted for his life. He was to get more than he would ever be able to scheme for.

- Though we refrain from being dogmatic, but we offer that the dream was foundational to Jacob's understanding of Joseph who would become the archetypical dreamer in the family and in the biblical story. When Joseph the eleventh son of Jacob began to dream, Joseph got into all kinds of trouble. He shared his dreams with his father and his brothers and while Jacob wondered on the meaning of the dreams, the brothers became so resentful of him that they found opportunity to get rid of him by first throwing him into a pit and later selling him to Midianite traders, who took him to Egypt where they sold him into Egyptian slavery. We are to say much more on this, but here we merely note that he lived by the power of his dreams and never gave up, until he became one of the most respectable governors this world has ever known. Because of living by his dream, Joseph was able to save his father Jacob and his whole family from starvation during a seven year famine that was to overtake the whole region of Egypt and its neighboring lands. As we might learn from Jacob's dream, so in Joseph's dreams we can learn much about the following: personal discovery, destination, direction, life's decisions, personal dedication, determination, discipline, daring, doing, diligence, dependability, development, discernment, dignity, and all the distinct descriptive words. His situations have helped us see what it means to bring a life to the ultimate goal that God has in store for humanity. Dreams are not to be taken lightly, for as we see God gives guidance to his people through dreams. The Bible says, "For God does speak—now one way, now another—though man may not perceive it. In a dream, in a vision of the night, when deep sleep falls on men as they slumber in their beds," (Job 33:14-15). In which case, it is our concern that anyone who wishes to be successful today should first seek the guidance of God.

Ask God to help you formulate your dream.

Ask God to help you use your dream to find a proper direction.

Ask God to help you use your dream to change your lifestyle.

We need to be careful about living a frivolous life like Jerome Kern suggests in his 1929 song, "Why was I born?" It was later popularized by Frank Sinatra and Ella Fitzgerald, A few lines in the song asks:

....

Why was I born
Why am I living
What do I get
What am I giving

Why do I want a thing
I daren't hope for
What can I hope for
I wish I knew

....

Why was I born?

....

The song might seem to be a dream of a love song with sweet words of nothing, but it also speaks to the more profound question of life being faced by many a person, "Why were they born? What are they doing here? Where are they going? This is not just for a class in Philosophy 101 or a High School first year class. It is stupid to think that "There is no set path to follow in life, just follow your heart." Every person in life needs to figure out a plan of action of life. Everyone needs a dream - a way to incubate the dream, a means of activating the dream, a way to nurture the dream. All need to understand that entering in the game of life, means that you should not only have a plan for yourself but that God has a plan for your life and that the best path of life is to integrate your plans with God's plan. Such is the story of Joseph. His dreams seemed wild and misunderstood, but he came to learn of God's plan in his life, and although there were twists and turns, yet he came to realize the best of his dream.

Mapping Your Life's Dream(s)

Dreaming is tracing life's paths with a future orientation. It is living the game of life, as if we are playing baseball or softball or any other game. We call dreaming **Life Maps Legacy**, because we believe that every step we take in our life's dream leaves a path behind and makes a way to the future. We can retrace our steps when we follow a path. And we leave a path for others too. This guidebook is an aid for those who seek a tool to help them make it easier to find their way to their ultimate destination. Simple we are creating a framework that will help individuals who have the audacity to succeed. We are striving to enable people to ask with frankness:

Who they are?

What are they doing here?

Where are they going?

What are their dreams?

What are their commitments?

What are they worth?

How should they live?

How should they deal with failure?

How do they deal with success?

How one answers these questions may determine his or her successful or unsuccessful destiny. If individuals are ever to find out who they are and what they were meant to be, if they are ever to know their destiny, and their purpose in life, they will need **Life Maps**.

Life Maps have helped people like Hannibal to cross the Alps, Marco Polo to find China, Columbus to explore the Indies, and Huck Finn to tour the Mississippi. Life is a maze and those who enter in need **Life Maps** to succeed.

Dream it, believe it, and seek to achieve it

Think of any game that you have played, for example, *The Game of Life*. That is the board game that was created in the 1860s by Milton Bradley to help individuals on the path to success in jobs, marriage, the rearing of children, and other aspects of life. What did it feel like when you played? Some of the most popular ball games that are played around the world include:

Baseball – Softball- Basket ball- Football (and Soccer) -Paintball

Racquetball - Cricket (ball)- Golf (ball)- Tennis (ball)

All give us clues into life's successes or failures.

Did you know that every game can teach you something about your life and your dreams?

What game(s) do you play?

What has it taught you about life?

What does it teach about your ability for effective social interaction?

What has it taught you about yourself as an individual?

What demands has it placed on your life?

What skills have you learned from the game you played?

How have you dressed for the game you have played?

These are simple but serious questions that are really focused on our lives. They can help us with the discovery of our dreams. Of the games listed above let's discuss baseball. Baseball, because we believe that it speaks in a practical manner about dreams. Baseball is unique. It is one of those games where every ballpark is different. Baseball demands unique skills. In fact, it is said that football might be successful with a lot of brute force, but baseball demands a lot of skill and wisdom. Baseball demands profound discipline. It teaches us how to focus and how to turn failures into successes. It is called a game of failures. It demands patience. It is a game of dreams. It is a game of discovery. It is a game of destiny. It is a game that teaches how one is to make effective decisions. It is a game that demands profound dedication. It is a game of daring, a game of discipline, a game of determination, development, discernment and dignity. It is a game that teaches much about distraction, dissuasion and doubt. If you play it with negative thoughts you are on the road to failure. If you play it with positive thoughts, that is half the road to success. The great baseball player, Yogi Berra is given a lot of credit for interesting quotes that seem to contradict the logical construction of discourse. Here is one: "90% of the game is half mental." Hockey player Jim McKenny says it more logically, "Half the game is mental; the other half is being mental." Of course, you cannot just think about it- you need to play to succeed. This is why we call this guide a manual. Our wish is that those who use it will engage it, doing the exercises with their hands, feet, hearts, soul and everything. The point we will be making over and over again is that success not only demands a dream or a vision, or personal confidence, but total commitment. Again we are using baseball as the underlay of life's game; we have seen that in baseball as in some other games, one has to be completely committed every moment, or else he will surely fail and never be restored.

The point of this discussion is to talk about dreaming – that is to focus on the way that we think and how our thinking impacts our behavior. We are continuing questions such as:

Do you have a life's dream?

How is your dream being constructed?

Does your dream have a focus?

Is your dream mere fantasy? Or does it have connection with reality?

Check your dream. See where it leads.

Sholom Aleichem says, "Life is a dream for the wise, a game for the fool, a comedy for the rich, a tragedy for the poor."

WHO DO YOU THINK YOU ARE?

Many people who are going through life have no blueprint or map of life, and so they end up in despair. They wish to be successful but they want to turn wherever their minds lead to get to home base before they get on first base. They want to be on home base before running the bases. They have no plan for their game or any idea of how to get to their destination. They are therefore not able to deal with failures, frustrations, anxieties, hardships and the many other negatives that are encountered in the games of life. They invariably do not understand who they are, what they need to be doing, and where they need to go. In such cases, they are not able to make the necessary changes to get themselves to the end of their journey.

One game that has taught us a lot about the map of life is baseball. Baseball is called "A metaphor of life." It is known as the game that transformed American social history. Babe Ruth shared a particular bias when he said, "Baseball was, is and always will be to me the best game in the world."

The story of Jackie Robinson, the first black man who integrated the Majors, is well known. We will reference Robinson in one of our presentations, but here, the point which we intend is that baseball has been a helpful game to teach us about social transformation and how it might impact destination. Although we cannot say that we are the greatest fans of the game, we discovered that the game became a wonderful means of building relationship with our three sons when they were quite young, and especially when they were young adolescents. We became attracted to baseball since the days when we lived in the Bronx. Of course, since our sons got tagged to the Yankees we chose the Mets. We argued about the trades and performance of players and many other subjects concerning their life's development. As we watched many games we took notes about the sense of purpose for teams and players, and the amount of discipline that was demanded of professional players. As we tried to understand the game, we talked about Little League, Spring Training, and the struggle to enter into the Majors. We also talked about such elements of the game as pitching, batting, base running, fielding, umpiring, coaching, managing, and preparing for road trips. We tried to learn the names of players, managers, coaches, and teams and studied their personalities, capabilities, skills, attitudes, actions and characters, on and off the field. We do not think we know that much about baseball, but we think we have discovered some reasons why some players are so successful while others are not. Baseball is a game that helps us with self-discovery. It teaches us much about life.

Read the following life story and share with a peer what three significant lessons you have learned from the story.

Bernabé Williams and Self-Discovery

One Major League Baseball player that we followed for several years was Bernie Williams (Bernabé Figueroa Williams). He was known as one of the Yankees most outstanding outfielders. Before coming to baseball, Bernie was active in track and field - winning medals at an international meet at the age of 15. He was one of the world's best 400-meter runners for his age. On his 17th birthday, September 13, 1985, Bernie signed a professional contract with the New York Yankees organization. Playing for the Yankees' AA team in Albany, he continued to develop his athletic skills particularly in the coveted area of switch-hitting. Although Yankee management viewed him as a great prospect, his rise to the Majors was delayed by the solid outfield that the team had developed in the early 1990s. Nevertheless, he managed to break into the Majors in 1991 to replace the injured Roberto Kelly for the second half of that season. Finding this opportunity, Bernie did as best he could, but he only batted .238 in 320 at bats and was demoted to the minors until Danny Tartabull was injured. His return to the Majors gave him another opportunity and he worked much harder than the first. This time he put up solid numbers. During the 1998 season, in which the Yankees went 114-48 to set a then American League regular season record, Bernie finished with a .339 average, and he became the first player to win a batting title, Gold Glove award, and World Series ring in the same year. After the 1998 season, Bernie landed a 7-year, $87.5-million contract with the Yankees, one of the largest in baseball at the time. For the length of his contract, the Yankees made the playoffs every single year, and as a result, Bernie continued to add to his postseason statistics—being placed in the top 10 of various career postseason categories. He also carved a place in the Yankee record books, placing him in the elite company of former Yankee greats.

Bernie's contract with the Yankees expired at the end of the 2006 season. After having sat out the entire 2007 season, Bernie's career as a Major League player was over. It is a great inspiration to see Bernie with his guitar on varied TV channels. His guitar playing is a second career. Whatever else might be said of him, it can be said, here is a young man who sought in every way to discover who he was, and once he found himself, he went to work to accomplish his dream. The inspirational statement he made at the end of his Major League career carries profound significance. (With some modifications, the biography of Bernie Williams was taken from Wikipedia).

QUESTIONS THAT WILL HELP YOU TO DISCOVER YOUR GAME PLAN FOR LIFE

WHAT AM I DOING HERE?

THIS IS ABOUT MY LIFE'S MISSION

WHO AM I?

THE IS ABOUT IDENTITY

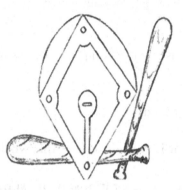

WHERE AM I GOING

THIS IS ABOUT MY VISION

What is your personality like?
What are your best life skills?
What do you like to do without being asked?
What are people saying you are good at?
What are you not good at?
What is your learning style?
Have you ever tried to map your mind?
Do you have a life coach?

The previous questions are not optional. They must be faced squarely as each person navigates his or her game of life.

Sooner or later, everyone must recognize that life cannot be lived by the flip of a coin. Life must be discovered and lived.

Some answers will be easy, others quite difficult. But we must investigate our lives and find the right answers.

Some answers will be more helpful to us, some more helpful to others. But they are beneficial, for when we know the answers, others might be able to help us get along.

In every answer one needs the help of God. We have heard it said, "God helps those who help themselves." While there is no complete truth in it, yet it has a point of validity. One cannot just pray for success and sit back waiting for it. Such a person would be called a sloth – a worthless person. Success demands passion, prayer and work.

Read the biblical book of *Ecclesiastes* as soon as you get a chance and notice what it says about the map for your life.

Notice what it says about life without God.

Look at what it says about the life that is built on a mere **this worldly achievement**.

Underline a few of the key words such as **generations, wind, sun, gain, profit**, and see what meaning they bring to you.

Now read the following proverbs and see how they correspond with what you have read in Ecclesiastes.

Proverbs 19:21 affirms that all the planning and investigations of the human mind exist to accomplish the purpose of God in the world.

Proverbs 16:3 commands us to commit our work to the Lord in the confidence that He will put our plans on a firm foundation.

Proverbs 21:5 "The plans of the diligent lead surely to abundance."

Proverbs 24:27 sounds like a mother advising the child "Plan your work and work your plan."

After reading the passages and answering the questions above, how would you define success?

MAPPING YOUR LIFE

A Life Map shows us the best road or strategic direction we might choose to get to a specific destination in our life. Often enough, there are many roads or strategic directions that we can employ to get to a destination. However, any person of wisdom who seeks a successful destination, is not overly concerned about the shortest road or longest road; such a person is most concerned about the best road. Such a person will therefore ask, what is the best road to take? Not the easiest road. What obstacles might I have to face on the road? Are there detours on the road? What hills, valleys, mountains, plateaus or other features are on the road? How might I navigate the road?

Knowing ourselves

Knowing the road is one thing, but knowing your capacity to negotiate the road is another thing. Life maps are designed to help individuals know who they are and where they are on the road. From a strategic perspective, they help us build the story of our life's journey.

Who we are is determined by the following questions.

1. What are our capabilities?

2. What are our potentials?

3. Do we have any special gifts?

4. How do we think?

5. How do we learn?

6. How effective do we organize ourselves?

7. What tactics do we use to realize who we are?

8. What principles do we have for the regulation of our lives?

9. What are our guidelines for charting our life's direction?

Even with the sophistication of Global Positioning Systems (GPS) we have to contend with these crucial questions in order to be clear about where we are heading

1. How clearly do we perceive the destination?

2. How well do we plan for the future?

3. How well do we follow directions?

4. How effective is our capacity for decision-making?

5. How well do we listen?

6. How much are we willing to learn?

Being ourselves?

Great worlds stand before us, but we cannot know them except we venture into them. Our successes depend on how well we use the right road maps. In his book, *Spiritual Leadership*, J. Oswald Sanders discusses some essential qualities of leadership. He makes the point that Jesus trained His disciples for their future roles by taking them "on the road." He emphatically states, "Jesus did not ask the twelve to sit down and take notes in a formal classroom. Jesus' classrooms were the highways of life; His principles and values came across in the midst of daily experiences. Jesus placed the disciples in internships (Luke 10:17-24) that enabled them to learn through failure and success (Mark 9:14-29). He delegated authority and responsibility to them; they were able to bear it. Jesus's wonderful teaching in John 13-16 was their graduation address." (p. 51).

Road trips are a very important aspect of development to baseball teams. When a team is going on the road, it reviews what is involved in the rigors of the road, then prepares itself (physically, emotionally, and mentally), for the trip. The preparation takes into account such things as pre-departure planning, setting the hours of leaving and arriving, thinking of the kinds of stadia in which it will play, focusing on leadership vision, team building, priorities, decisions and choices, direction, determination, diligence, responsibility, character development, self-control, encouragement, cooperation, respecting authority, integrity and a whole lot more. The point is to create a frame for winning. In effect, if a team knows how to win on the road, such a team might have the stamina to win at home, and consequently, the possibility of a successful season. Here are a few questions and comments about teams that win on the road:

Do you agree that, *"Success breeds more success as this team plays solid baseball on the road?"*

"This will be a test for success on the road for this team."

"Winning on the road can be a key ingredient to success for that number one position."

"Will the . . . road success lately catch on and help this team increase their lead?"

"The road success lately. . . could very well help their confidence level?"

"You may have noticed a pattern of the teams that have been successful on the road lately. Five of the six teams are leading their division and the other team is in second place. Follow these teams and how they are doing on the road."

What have you discovered about the teams that are winning on the road in contrast to the teams that are not winning on the road?

Yes, we talk about "The road" as if it is the only thing that counts, but the destination (that is the end of the road) is also very important.

Distinguishing ourselves?

Which is more important, the journey or the destination?

Have you ever seen a sign that says, "Journey to Nowhere?"

Have you ever seen an art display that says, "Driving without destination?"

One thing we have learned from watching baseball and life in general, is that one cannot be successful if one never touches HOME PLATE.

Of course, one should not say that the journey is not important. To say it is not about the destination, but it is about the journey, is to go down a path of despair.

Whether you are eight, eighteen, or eighty, you can still live with the excitement of a dream and a sense of destiny.

In his book *Your Road Map for Success: You Can Get There From Here*, Dr. John Maxwell says,

> "Some people live their lives from day to day, allowing others to dictate what they do and how they do it. They never discover their true purpose for living. Others know their purpose, yet never act on it. They are waiting for inspiration or permission or an invitation to get started. . . ." (p. 13).

Are you ready to start on the road of life? Explain.

_____

_____

What do you need to know to get where you want to go?

- One cannot be afraid to explore the road. You cannot practice the skills of the road in a parking lot.

- Success does not just happen at the end of the road, but is built on little steps or stages along the road.

- Failure on the road does not mean that one cannot reach a successful end.

- Detours on the road give one opportunities to re-read one's map, refocus, rethink, reorganize and refine one's strategies for the road.

- No journey is ever successfully completed without sacrifice and suffering on the road: "No pain, no gain."

- It is not how quickly one gets to the end of a journey that counts. It is the persistence that leads to the end the journey.

- There is more to life than being on the road.

WORDS OF WISDOM

"Remember that ambition alone will not get you anywhere.
You need to stay away from paths of destruction.
And since you never have total control of the way that you must travel,
Learn how to negotiate your road with God."

– D. Robert Kennedy

GOD CALLS US TO OVERREACH OURSELVES BECAUSE HIS REACH IS SO MUCH LARGER THAN OURS – JOHN EGMOND HAGGAI.

CHOOSE THE HIGH ROAD

Life never gives us the chance of going down two roads simultaneously, so we have need to choose which is the right road for our lives. Which road will you choose?

THE ROAD NOT TAKEN

TWO roads diverged in a yellow wood,
And sorry I could not travel both
And be one traveler, long I stood
And looked down one as far as I could
To where it bent in the undergrowth;

Then took the other, as just as fair,
And having perhaps the better claim,
Because it was grassy and wanted wear;
Though as for that the passing there
Had worn them really about the same,

And both that morning equally lay
In leaves no step had trodden black.
Oh, I kept the first for another day!
Yet knowing how way leads on to way,
I doubted if I should ever come back.

I shall be telling this with a sigh
Somewhere ages and ages hence:
Two roads diverged in a wood, and I—
I took the one less traveled by,
and that has made all the difference

Robert Frost

The Path of Delight

The Way to Destruction

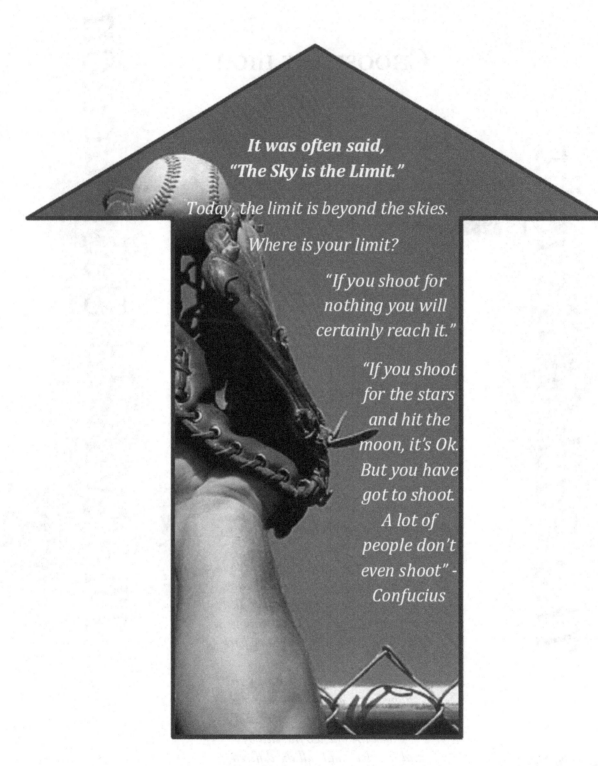

*It was often said,
"The Sky is the Limit."*

Today, the limit is beyond the skies.

Where is your limit?

*"If you shoot for
nothing you will
certainly reach it."*

*"If you shoot
for the stars
and hit the
moon, it's Ok.
But you have
got to shoot.
A lot of
people don't
even shoot" -
Confucius*

LEARN HOW TO RESIST THE POWER OF GRAVITY

Do The Following Activities That Might Help To Coalesce Your Dream

ACTVITY I – ACTIVITY IS THE LAW OF LIFE

Write two statements for each of the following.

What inspiration does the picture on the previous page bring to you concerning your effort to resist the power of gravity?

1. _____

2. _____

ACTIVITY II – A PERSONALITY INVENTORY TEST

Take a personality test and try to understand what personality type you are? There are numerous such tests online. You might choose to do the Myers Briggs Temperament Index which offers about 16 personality mixes. Or you might take some simpler tests that focus on the four personality types - Choleric, Sanguine, Melancholic or Phlegmatic. Pay special attention to the two traits – introverted or extroverted - identified with the personalities. Which traits affect you most? How would such traits affect you if you were a baseball player? How might you relate to a crowd? How might you relate to criticism and so on? See example in Appendix IV

ACTIVITY III – A TALENT INVENTORY TEST

Take a talent test. There are many such tests on the internet. A talent test seeks to identify what natural abilities you were born with. How would your natural abilities make you a good or great baseball player? You will need to remind yourself that talent is 50% of what will make you successful. See example in Appendix V

ACTIVITY IV – A GIFT TEST

Take a gift test. Gifts are different from talents. Talents are considered natural, gifts are considered supernatural. Gifts are given to us by God. The great baseball pitcher Nolan Ryan said, "My ability to throw a baseball was a gift. It was a God-given gift. And I am truly appreciative of that gift. It took me a while to figure that out … and when I finally did, I dedicated myself to be the best pitcher I possibly could be, for as long as I possibly could be."

Note: It is very important to take note that no matter how powerful your personality, your talent or gift, if all is not dedicated to God, you will not be as effective as you might be on the road of life.

GOD'S MAP FOR DISCOVERING YOUR LIFE'S DREAM

See how Joseph discovered himself

It is said that "A person who follows God is always on the right path." Thus after reading the biblical story of Joseph (Genesis 37, 39-50) we took note of how well it illustrates Joseph's awareness of a divine sense of destiny. He lived his life with an immense dream and a compelling desire to follow God's path. He was called a dreamer. His father had already decided that he was to be the family's heir. Being the first son of Rachael, his favorite wife, Jacob gave Joseph a princely coat of many colors. As Joseph later shared his dreams, his father sensed in it a prophetic vision of leadership. Of course, his father took time to question why he, being father, would also have to bow down to Joseph, according to his dream. But Father Jacob could not grasp totally how Joseph was to reach his destiny. Joseph's brothers also sensed that Joseph was different, but it was hard for them to accept the difference and so they became resentful and bitter toward him. Of course, part of the reason for the resentment was that Joseph would always "call out" his brothers when they went wrong. He would report them to their father, and they hated him. When his father sent him into the field to visit his brothers, their resentment and bitterness grew to such an extent that their only thought was of killing him. Subsequently one of the brothers convinced the other brothers to place him into a slime pit. But later while that brother was

> *And Joseph dreamed a dream, and he told it to his brethren: and they hated him yet the more.*

away from the scene they all decided that it was better to sell him to a band of Midianite traders who took him into Egypt where he was sold into slavery.

The direction that Joseph's life took in Egypt is of interest. It was a time when Joseph was to discover himself. Through enslavement and imprisonment, he was ultimately brought before Pharaoh and appointed to become Governor of Egypt. The way that most Bible commentators and the Koran speak of Joseph, in the revelation he made to his brothers, when, during the great famine they visited Egypt, is of interest. Instead of speaking of it as a moment of revelation they speak of it as a moment of "discovery." In what we might call the most intriguing moment of encounter with the brothers, he said, "I am Joseph, your brother." (Genesis 45:5). One has to read the full story of Joseph's life to understand what led to this declaration. We are not going to do that now, since we will have several opportunities to reflect upon it, but here are two interesting notes:

1. One comes from a reflection by Pastor Dr. David Fisher (2007) who says, "Joseph's life is part of a sordid, twisted family drama. It's a story that features greed, avarice, jealousy, violence, sex, power politics, and palace intrigue. Ten chapters long the Joseph story is a disturbing tale about some very disturbing people – very ordinary people. And in it all God was at work – writing straight with crooked lines!"

2. The other point flows from the understanding that Joseph had to pass through the experiences he did in order to acknowledge his arrogance, moral superiority, jealousy and bitterness. While his older brothers were subjected to the hard work of taking care of the sheep, he had the privilege of remaining at home receiving his father's intimate care. Instead of simply appreciating his privileges, he found opportunities to taunt his brothers and make them angry. While we might not excuse the way in which the brothers treated him, we cannot fail to see that Joseph had a developing character and attitude that needed to be corrected if he were to be the great governor of Egypt that he was to become. However, in order to get on the corrective path he needed, he had to "discover himself." He needed to know who he was. What he was doing on earth and where he was to go with his life.

The real point is that Joseph had to discover who he was as he came to know the will of God. Joseph evidently came to the understanding of the will of God through dreams and visions and by his personal connection with God. His life is recorded in the Bible, so we will review his life from the Bible. However our interest is not only historical, but practical. That is to say, we wish that in a contemporary the life of Joseph can serve as inspiration to help us discover our goals for the game of life. If you have been to church for even a short time, you've probably heard the minister emphasizing Bible study. So you might ask "Is Bible study really that important?" Isn't attending church services every week enough? We answer to the latter question, No! For thousands of years now, there is the clearest recognition that the Bible is a wonderful source of wisdom. It tells us where we are coming from, what we need to be doing here and how to prepare for the future. The Bible is not just a book about behavior; it is a book about life. It helps us to find meaning and purpose in life. It helps us to know the will of God. The Bible is the book which constantly reminds us that life is not all about the here and now, but is about eternity. It tells us that success is not only what we can achieve in this life, but in the life to come. These we feel are good reasons to use it as our Life Map.

Summary: The point of this discussion was to help you know yourself.

Who are you? What are your dreams?

What is your personality like? Are you fearful or are you courageous?

What are your abilities? Are you willing to think about them?

Write a note to yourself stating what you have discovered about yourself and what you wish to do with your life from now on.

_____

_____

_____

_____

_____

_____

_____

_____

_____

_____

_____

DESTINATION

"Clarity of vision is the key to achieving your dream once you've discovered it."

– Leo Babauta (2007)

THE END GAME: ACHIVING YOUR DREAM

Anyone who plays or watches a season of 162 games of baseball, or a season of any other game knows that the success of the season is not just in the number of games played. That may be quite important, but the ultimate is what happens in the end game. Only a few individuals remember those teams that did not play in the end game – end of season. Those who play the game might wish to forget the season themselves if they have not played in the end game. As each game is played, it tells a lot about where the season is intended to go. It tells a lot about destination.

As you participate in the game of life, think very clearly of your end game. At the end of each game, or a season, effective baseball managers and coaches evaluate their plays to see what they did right or what they did wrong. Whenever they lose a game they study carefully what were the bad plays. When they win a game they evaluate what they did well to get their team to the next level until they reach the championship. There is very rarely a perfect game, but every game has to end. The lessons to be remembered as one reflects on the game of baseball are:

> *There is no celebration without a clear sense of destiny*

1. Baseball players who reach a successful destination have an excellent **sense of vision** – usually they test 20/20.

2. Baseball players who reach a successful destination know how to **focus** – they know how to concentrate on their goal and not be distracted by the crowd.

3. Baseball players who reach a successful destination learn how to **predict the future**. For example, successful batters use their experiences of past situations to predict the next pitch. In which case, they can prepare how to hit the next ball, which often comes to them in four tenths of a second.

What we want to do, in this aspect of our study is to clearly define what should be your vision or end game – destination. In referencing the Iraq war, Senator Richard Shelby stated, "If there's not any end game, we're in quicksand. We take one more step, and we're still there, and there's no way out."

Read the following life story and share with a peer what three significant lessons you have learned from the Cy Young's life.

CY Young – A Man on a Mission

One's humble birth does not determine whether one will succeed or not. We can learn a great lesson from Denton True Young who was born in Gilmore, a small farming community in Washington Township, New Jersey, on March 29, 1867 and died November 4, 1955. He attended school up until the 6th grade. He dropped out of school to help on the family farm. At the end of each day he would play baseball. As he developed he played for many amateur baseball leagues. In 1888 he pitched and played second base with the Carrollton team. His performance was so impressive that at the end of the season, he received an offer to play for the Canton team. The offer launched his career as a professional player. In 1889 Young began his professional life with the Canton League – a professional minor league. He later entered the Majors in which he continued his career until his final season in 1911. During his career he won 511 games and lossed 316 with an ERA of 2.63 and wrapping up 2,803 strikeouts, which is a .617 winning percentage. Because of the velocity of his balls he was nicknamed CY Young, coined by his team mates and reporters from the word "Cyclone". We hear today of the Cy Young award and might never think of the guy who started out his career as a wild pitcher, but who was so determined to win that he became one of the best controlled pitchers in baseball. He had his life's goals and reached them. Sportswriter Ogden Nash says of him:

"Y is for Young
The magnificent Cy;
People batted against him,
But I never knew why." (With some modifications, the biography of Cy Young was taken from Wikipedia).

"A man has to have goals - for a day, for a lifetime - and that was mine, to have people say, 'There goes Ted Williams, the greatest hitter who ever lived."

– Ted Williams

ACTIVITY I

_____

1. Finish the following with a statement that might tell the destination you wish to go with your life.

   I am going to

   _____

2. Predict what might happen to you in the next three years based on the destination you have chosen

   _____

3. What are you doing right now that might help you get to your future destination.

   _____

4. How **passionate** are you about getting to the destination you have chosen?

   ____ Not passionate ____ Somewhat passionate ____ Very passionate

ACTIVITY II

How can the following fit into your plans to reach your destination.

   Put "H "for those that are high priority in your life and "L" for those which are low.

1. Working at a donut shop ____

2. Having meaning in my life ____

3. Getting a sports model car ____

4. Going to school/College ____

5. Maintaining a healthy body ____

6. Playing basket ball on the street corner ____

7. Building a successful relationship ____

8. Being successful at any cost ____

9. Working at a clothing store ____

10. Having a good time with friends ____

CHECK YOUR FEELINGS ABOUT YOU

I believe I am the master of my own destiny.

I accept that no one can chart my life's course but me.

I know that no one can hold me back but me.

Do you believe these statements that follow?

1. It is not the destination, it is the journey. Yes ____ No ____

2. What you are going to be you are now becoming. Yes ____ No ____

3. I am a person who has a lot of personal confidence. Yes ____ No ____

4. I trust others to help me get to where I want to go. Yes _____ No _____

5. Dream lofty dreams, and as you dream, so shall you be. Yes _____ No _____

6. Dreams are the seedlings of realities. Yes _____ No _____

7. More often than not our best desires receive our greatest attention. Yes _____ No _____

REFLECT:

Look at all the responses that you have given in Activity II. Do you think you have the mindset that will allow you to reach the end of your journey? Why or why not?

Write a sentence to explain your response.

_____

_____

ACTIVITY III

Finish the following sentences and then evaluate how you feel

1. Going to school helps _____

2. Having a happy family makes me _____

3. Gaining a profession _____

4. Going to church _____

5. Becoming a great leader _____

6. Being a respected person _____

7. Being a successful person _____

8. Being a confident person _____

9. Being a person with calm attitude _____

10. Owning an expensive cell phone _____

11. Owning an expensive late model car _____

12. Having a lot of money _____

Answer "yes" or "no" to the following questions then briefly explain your response

1. Do you ever feel like you are in a fog of uncertainty? ____ ____

2. Do you ever feel like you are searching for clear signals for your life? ____ ____

Just about everyone has faced uncertainty and the need for clear signals, but the ones who are effective at resolving problems are the ones who are on their way to a successful destination. From our baseball scenario which was given at the start of our present discussion, we note three points of importance on reaching a successful destination.

1. Learning to focus

2. Keeping the focus

3. Finishing with the focus

Evaluate what you think the following sayings tell about your sense of destination

"In all undertakings it is necessary to consider the end" – La Fontaine

_____

"The end of a dissolute life is commonly a desperate death" – Anonymous

_____

_____

"That the birds of worry and care fly above your head, this you cannot change, but that they build nests in your hair, this you can prevent." - Chinese Proverb

_____

_____

"The number one reason that people don't get what they want is that they do not know what they want."

– T. Havre Eker

_____

_____

Choose a topic for a book you would like to write about yourself such as:

Life without dreams
Playing without dreams
Fielding without dreams
Dreams! Dreams! Dreams!
Or another topic
Write a one-paragraph introduction to the book.

GOD'S MAP FOR YOUR LIFE'S DESTINATION

Joseph, the eleventh son of Jacob, was a young man with a powerful sense of destiny. He constantly spoke of his dreams. It was not only his passion and desires, or what his father wanted for him, but his destiny was scripted by God. Aside from Pharaoh, Joseph was to become the most powerful man of the world in his time. It has been said that Joseph's destiny was to save his family from starvation and hence save the nation of Israel from complete annihilation. In addition, Joseph saved the Egyptians and other nations that came to him for help.

In order to prepare Joseph for his destiny, he was put through a series of tests. We will mention the tests at varied stages in future reflections, but what is significant here is to note that because Joseph passed each test he was able to achieve the destiny that God had prepared for him. God prepares us for our destiny by giving us dreams and visions. Someone says that God weighs each test to make sure that they are suited to us. The more weighty the destiny, the longer and harder the tests will be. It is the same when we prepare for any career or profession. If we want to achieve our destiny, we have to be willing to take and pass the tests. Have you ever wondered what your purpose is in life? Why are you here? Ask yourself, Have I ever taken a test, like Joseph? Please understand that your tests might lead you through hard times, heartaches, betrayal and difficulties. Your test might take some time to be completed. Can you imagine what Joseph was thinking for 13 years as a slave and a prisoner? Maybe he was asking God the very questions that you might be asking. If you are ever tempted to give in or give up, please don't give up like so many people do. If Joseph had given up during those 13 years, he would have completely missed his destiny. Maybe God would have found someone else. For sure God could! But it wouldn't have been Joseph. So, we are encouraged to keep moving forward, keep trusting, keep believing, keep dreaming, keep the passion high, keep following God and never give in or give up. Take a lesson from Joseph; learn from a person who attended the University of Hard Knocks. By overcoming multiple obstacles he found God's destiny for his my life, just as you can overcome and find the true destiny of your life. Joseph's destiny was not a matter of chance; it was in God's plan.

Your attitude determines your destiny.

Each person must take into serious consideration what will be his or her end.

The biblical book of ***Proverbs*** gives the advise, "My son, do not forget my teaching, but keep my commands in your heart, for they will prolong your life many years and bring you prosperity. Let love and faithfulness never leave you; bind them around your neck, write them on the tablet of your heart. Then you will win favor and a good name in the sight of God and man." Proverbs 3:1-4.

Yes, God has a plan for each life: Reflect on the following statements

"For I know the plans I have for you," declares the LORD, "plans to prosper you and not to harm you, plans to give you hope and a future." – Jeremiah 29: 11 NIV

"According to His own purpose and grace which was given to us in Christ Jesus before time began"- (2 Timothy 1:9).

"I will be a Father to you, and you shall be my sons and daughters, says the Lord Almighty" - 2 Corinthians 6:18. NRSV

Yes, each person must make a choice for life. What is your choice?

"He who sows wickedness reaps trouble" (Proverbs 22:8a). "All hard work brings a profit, but mere talk leads only to poverty" (Proverbs 14:23). "Do you want to be free from fear of the one in authority? Then do what is right and he will commend you" (Romans 13:3)

"Many live as enemies of the cross of Christ. Their destiny is destruction" (Philippians 3:18-19). "This is the fate of those who trust in themselves" (Psalm 49:13). It is wonderful when one chooses the divine destiny.

How can the following influence the choice of your destination? Check all that you think are crucial. Be sure you can justify all that you have checked.

1. Family _____

2. Friends _____

3. Connectivity – Network _____

4. Opportunities _____

5. Commitments _____

6. Conviction _____

7. Passion _____

8. Parents _____

9. Willingness to work hard _____

10. Wealth _____

Explain how the following statements can affect the chances of your choices in life.

A. *"… the values of the world we inhabit and the people we surround ourselves with have a profound effect on who we are."* – Malcolm Gladwell – *Outliers*

_____

_____

_____

B. *"Goals provide the energy source that powers our lives. One of the best ways we can get the most from the energy we have is to focus it. That is what goals can do for us; concentrate our energy."* – Denis Waitley

_____

_____

_____

_____

_____

_____

"Having conceived of his purpose, a man should mentally mark out a straight pathway to achievement, looking neither to the right nor to the left."

– James Allen

"The will to do, stems from the knowledge that we can do." - James Allen

"There can be no progress, no achievement without sacrifice . . . . " - James Allen

*"There is a divine purpose determining the path of our lives. There is no chance in a good **person's [gender change mine]** life"* – F. B. Meyer

Here is what the Bible says:

"Before I formed you in the womb I knew you, before you were born I set you apart; I appointed you as a prophet to the nations" (Jeremiah 1:4-5).

"There is no wisdom, no insight, no plan that can succeed against the LORD"   (Proverbs 21:30).

"The lot is cast into the lap, but its every decision is from the LORD" (Proverbs 16:33).

"The king's heart is in the hand of the LORD; he directs it like a watercourse wherever he pleases" (Proverbs 21:1).

'No eye has seen, no ear has heard, / no mind has conceived / what God has prepared for those who love him"(1 Corinthians 2:7-9).

If God takes you seriously enough to entrust you with a vision, then you must take yourself seriously. – John Edmund Haggai

"If you have the opportunity to play this game of life you need to appreciate every moment. A lot of people don't appreciate the moment until it's passed." - Kanye West

"When we make a mess of life it is because we fail to follow God's plan

for our lives." – D. Robert Kennedy

Look at the Diamond below and write a sentence under each idea that focuses on your life's destination.

IS YOUR LIFE DIRECTED TO AN ULTIMATE GOAL?

DOES YOUR LIFE HAVE A PURPOSE?

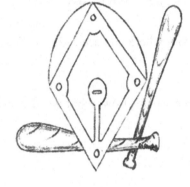

IS YOUR GOAL A FANTASY?

Do you like what you have seen?
After you look back at the things you have seen concerning the focus and target of your life, respond to the questions on the next page that truly describe where you are going.

TRANSFORMING YOUR ROAD MAP

1. Describe how you see yourself at the moment, in terms of your movement towards your destination. Here are some questions to focus your mind.

    If you could slip into the back of the place where your own funeral was being conducted, with no one seeing you, what would you like them to be saying? What are they saying? Is what you are hearing what you would like them to be saying? If you do not like what they are saying, what would you like them to say?

2. Where would you like to go from where you are right now? Use the following hint to help you.

    If you could see yourself 10 years from now, what would you like to see yourself doing?

3. What do you see as the greatest obstacle affecting your progress towards where you wish to go?

4. What are your strengths that can help to keep you on the road where you wish to go?

5. What do you consider your weaknesses in focusing on your destination?

6. What kind of help do you need to stay on the road to your destination?

"God has given each of us our "marching orders'. Our purpose here on Earth is to find those orders and carry them out. Those orders acknowledge our special gifts."

- Soren Kierkegaard

WORDS TO PONDER

Imagine yourself wanting to be a baseball player and someone says, "With your skill set, you have no hope," but your mindset is that you can do it. Think of some of the things that you might need to do in achieving your goal. Think of what risks you might need to take. What have you done in your life thus far to help you along the way? What have you learned from your experiences of the past? Never forget that there are persons who have been told the same things as you have been told, and they have become some of the greatest achievers in their fields of choice. Of course, it is true that in every field, sometimes with our best efforts, our skill sets do not match our goals. In such a case, there is no need to feel like a failure, but what you need is to learn how to transition to a field that is as stimulating. You cannot play baseball but you might be able to play basketball, golf, or other games.

Summary: The point of this discussion is to help you find your destination. Finish the following sentences

My end point is

My greatest goal in life is to

I cannot visualize my goal now, but I sure

Yesterday is a cashed check and cannot be negotiated. Tomorrow is a promissory note and cannot yet be utilized. Today is cash in hand. Spend it wisely. - Anonymous

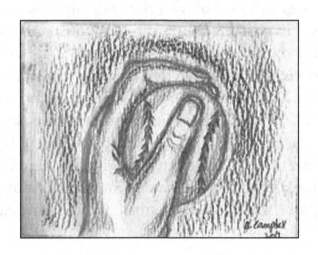

"How you played in yesterday's game is all that counts."

- Jackie Robinson

DIRECTION

"Go confidently in the direction of your dreams! Live the life you've imagined. As you simplify your life, the laws of the universe will be simpler."

- Henry David Thoreau

WHERE DO YOU THINK YOU ARE GOING?

When you play baseball, in fact, any game, the key to success is following the directions-- the rules of the game. Procedural violations will get you into trouble. You might cheat your way through a game and win, but you cannot win by cheating all the time. It is especially important to follow the rules when you have to play for a whole season. The rules of preparation, the rules of healthy habits and the rules for playing the game must be taken into deep consideration. Staying up late at night, failing to exercise to strengthen the muscles, eating the wrong kinds of foods, drinking a lot of alcohol, smoking and using drugs are all outside the rules of the game. Often enough, the rules are not all written in a book, but they are built into the game itself. Just as there are rules for a game, so also there are rules for travel. In order for a trip to be successful, one needs to know the rules of the road. You can't run red lights, stop signs, cross-streets and crosswalks and expect to stay alive. The rules of a game and the rules of the road are important.

> *There is no celebration without following directions*

Read the following life story and share with a peer what three significant lessons you have learned from the story.

Joe Torre- A Man of Purpose

One baseball player that represents one who understands the rules of the game very well is Joe Torre. Joseph Paul Torre, known as one of baseball's premier managers, managed the Los Angeles Dodgers and also the New York Yankees from 1996-2007. Under his leadership, the Yankees reached the post season each year and won ten American League East Division titles, six American League pennants, four World Series titles, and overall compiled a .605 winning percentage. With 2,246 wins (through the end of the 2009 season), he currently ranks 5th in all-time Major League Baseball all-time managerial wins.

His managerial success, particularly his achievements with the Yankees, has led many commentators to predict Torre to be a first-ballot Baseball Hall of Famer upon his eligibility.

Torre followed in his brother Frank's footsteps and joined the Milwaukee Braves in 1960. He quickly became a reliable player with the veteran Braves team which included Hank Aaron and Eddie Mathews. He was primarily a catcher, but also spent significant time as a first baseman. In 1965, Torre won a Gold Glove as a catcher. In an article for the *St. Petersburg Independent* that year, *Beat Generation* author Jack Kerouac called Torre "the best catcher since Roy Campanella." After moving to Atlanta, he hit .315 in 1966. Torre was traded to St. Louis in 1969 in exchange for Orlando Cepeda. He continued as a catcher for his first two seasons with the Cardinals, but became primarily a third baseman in 1971. That was the best year of his career; he hit .363 and drove in 137 runs en route to the National League MVP award. Torre was traded to the Mets in 1975 for Ray Sadecki and Tommy Moore. He became a player-coach, then a player-manager before retiring.

What makes Joe Torre so effective as a manager, and as a player, is the fact that he knows and understands the fundamentals of the game. He has a game plan and follows the plan. He is a man who could take direction and is now able to give them. He takes into account, not only the rules of the game, but, the uniqueness of each personality with whom he deals. His object is always to build an effective team with which to win. (With some modifications, the biography of Joe Torre was taken from Wikipedia).

> *"When I was a little boy, I wanted to be a baseball player and also join the circus. With the Yankees, I've accomplished both."*
>
> *- Craig Nettles*

WISE SAYINGS FOR THE ROAD OF LIFE

1. "If you don't know where you are going any road will get you there." - Lewis Carroll

2. "Direction is more important than speed. We are so busy looking at our speedometers that we forget the milestone." – Anonymous

3. "It is the direction and not the magnitude which is to be taken into consideration." - Thomas Payne

4. "I can't change the direction of the wind, but I can adjust my sail to always reach my destination." – Jimmy Dean

5. "If you do not change direction, you might end up where you are heading."– Lao Tzu

What directional changes do you think you need to make right now?

Check the emotions that truly express your mental state when you get on the road. Why do you think you feel the way you do. (What do you think trigger such feelings?)

1. Anxious		
2. Worried		
3. Stuck		
4. Restless		
5. Perplexed		
6. Frantic		
7. Focused		
8. Motivated		
9. Determined		
10. Driven		

According to your answers above, do you feel that your life has a direction, or are you one of those persons who finds yourself in a total state of confusion?

Yes _____ No _____ Not sure _____

In a sentence or two explain your answer _____

_____

_____

Have you ever gotten lost, missed your direction, or felt like you were spinning out of control?

_____

Explain what you did to regain your direction if you answered yes?

_____

1. Which of the following three strategies will lead you in the best direction of life?

     a. Letting things flow ____

     b. Creating a road map ____

     c. Setting some goals ____

2. Where do you see yourself three years from now?

_____

_____

3. Do you see any need to **change direction** so that you can fulfill your destiny?

     Certainly____ Maybe____ Not sure____

4. If you had to change directions, name three things that you would need to do.

_____

_____

_____

_____

ACTIVITY III

Someone asked a fifteen-year-old male, "What plans do you have for your life right now?" He answered without any thought, "None, I am just going with the flow."

PAIR SHARE

1. Discuss with a colleague the significance of the answer given above. Be sure to describe any dangers that you see in the answer.

2. Rate the list below on 1 - 10, (1 being the lowest and 10 being the highest) to explain your feelings about what seem to be among great deterrents to young men/women losing their direction in school these days.

    ☐ Fighting with girls or boys

☐ Using drugs

☐ Texting/sexting

☐ Playing basketball

☐ Eating – just eating

☐ Talking trash

☐ Smoking

☐ Listening to Hip Hop

☐ Assaulting security guards

☐ Disrespecting teachers

☐ Skipping classes

3. Check one or as many of the issues below that might be affecting your personal direction in life right now:

☐ Too many voices

☐ Too many angles

☐ Too many roads

☐ Too many choices

☐ Too few choices

☐ Too many opportunities

☐ Too few opportunities

☐ Too many advisors

☐ Too few advisors

☐ Too many counselors

☐ Too few counselors

☐ Too much information

☐ Lack of teachableness

☐ Being faithful

☐ Lack intuitiveness

☐ Too little passion for growth

☐ Not much desire to change

☐ Lack of personal confidence

Discuss with a peer, "How the following might help or impede the direction of any young man or woman."

Being too lethargic

Being too opinionated

Being too argumentative

Being too inaccessible

Being too distracted

Being too agitated

Being too prejudiced

In a brief paragraph state what were your conclusions.

_____

_____

_____

_____

_____

_____

FOCUS ON THE ROAD

GOD'S MAP FOR YOUR LIFE'S DIRECTION

Joseph: A Man of Direction

Joseph could not control everything about his life, but it is evident that from early in his life he had a well-defined sense of direction. Not only did he depend on his own smarts to get direction, but when he went to meet his brothers who were attending their flock in a distant place, he was willing to ask questions and take direction from a stranger when he was not sure of where to go. Read Genesis 45:15. Joseph left home and traveled to where he thought his brothers were. When he did not find them, he began to wander in the fields. A man found him, and figuring that he was lost sent him in the direction of Dothan where he would find his brothers. Joseph did not argue or question "what if," instead, he took the direction the man gave and found his brothers.

> *And he dreamed yet another dream, and told it his brethren.*

Of course, the full demonstration of Joseph's life as a man of direction came as a young adult of thirty years when he interpreted the dreams of King Pharaoh. Pharaoh had a dream about "the seven fat ears of corn and the seven lean ears; the seven fat cows and the seven lean ones ate the fat ones and were still lean. Joseph made it clear to the King that the meaning of the two dreams were the same, namely that Egypt would have seven years of abundant harvests and seven years of famine. On learning the meanings, Pharaoh appointed Joseph to the governorship of Egypt. Joseph then set forth a strategic plan on how to store grains from the seven years of abundance. For seven years he collected grains in silos. During the seven years of famine he sold the grains to the people so that there was no starvation in Egypt. Even the brothers, who sold him into slavery traveled to Egypt to buy grains. In his effort to bring his brothers to acknowledge their wrong and to establish his family in Egypt, Joseph showed how directed he was and that he was a strategic genius of planning. (Read the story in Genesis 41).

In speaking of the need for a clear sense of direction and planning in one's life, the greatest writer and collector of proverbs gives the following direction:

Following divine direction

Proverbs 3:5, 6: Trust in the Lord with all your heart and lean not on your own understanding; in all your ways acknowledge him, and he will make your paths straight. (NIV).

Following good advice

Proverbs 11:14: For lack of guidance a nation falls, but many advisers make victory sure. (NIV)

Look at the Diamond below and ask yourself about your life's direction.

DO YOU HAVE A MAP FOR YOUR LIFE?

DOES YOUR MAP MAKE CLEAR YOUR DIRECTION?

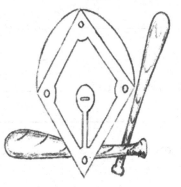

WHAT IS THE MOST PERSISTENT DIRECTION ON YOUR MAP?

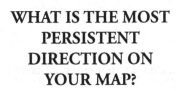

Do you like what you have seen?
After looking back at the things you have seen concerning your focus and management of your direction, respond to the questions on the next page that truly describe how effectively you follow direction.

TRANSFORMING YOUR ROAD MAP

1. How do you see yourself at the moment? Do you like who you are as you are? Do you like your habits, attitude? Do you like your personality and your character as you see them at the moment? In the space below, write a description of how you perceive yourself.

2. Which of the following steps might be most helpful to you in finding a proper direction for life?

   a   Remain focused on tasks _____

   b. Seek guidance from others _____

   c. Have a plan of action and stick to it _____

   d. Stop if you get tired _____

   e. Have several plans in mind _____

3. What do you see as the greatest obstacle affecting your progress at the moment?

4. Reflect on the direction you are now taking, and then say how it will help you to get to where you want to go.

5. What are some areas of weaknesses that can challenge you greatly, in your life's direction?

6. Who might be the best person to help you in finding your life's direction?

7. Reflect and answer "Yes" or "No" to each idea. Be ready to explain to a friend why you think.

   ❖ All your plans are leading in the right direction of life._____

   ❖ You have been listening to too many directions and is now confused._____

   ❖ The directional plans that you have laid out are perfect._____

   ❖ You have no need of support to carry out your plans._____

"If you do not change direction, you may end up where you are heading." - Lao Tzu

WORDS TO PONDER

For quite a few years you are in the Minor Leagues and you wish to go to the Majors. You feel like you are at a dead end and it is time for you to do some self-assessment. Are you too easily satisfied? Do you do things that will take you to the second and third base; things that will take you to home base? Do you have the skill while lacking the mentality to be an effective player? Whatever you are now thinking, remember what Joni Eareckson Tada, the woman who became a quadriplegic at the age of 17 said, *"We can't copy the world's slipshod way of looking at art – or life. If we want to have something of real worth and lasting value in our character, it won't come easy."*

Conclusion: The point of the discussion is to help you with a strategy for where your destination.

❖ A strategy contains the objectives and tactics to guide us in the direction we want to go.

❖ Do you have a strategy for determining where you want to go?

❖ A strategy will help you obey the rules so that you will not jump into disaster.

**IF YOU FOCUS ON THE RIGHT DIRECTION,
YOU WILL NEVER MISS THE WAY**

DECISION

"It's not hard to make decisions when you know what your values are."

- Roy Disney

HOW DO YOU THINK YOU WILL GET WHERE YOU NEED TO GO?

The capacity to make effective decisions is very critical for the outcome of baseball or any other game. Some games move at a slow pace and thus decisions are made slowly, while fast moving games allow for quick decisions. It is in a game that decision-making is vital. Often when thinking about decision-making, we (my wife and I) speak of how a baseball pitcher has to decide what pitches to make and when to make them. If the sequence, the batter will surely thrown, the best batters usually aspects of baseball one might the power of decisions are at the and player response on the field. is sent up to bat? Who plays field? These are critical questions

There is no celebration without effective decisions

wrong pitch is thrown in a benefit. If the right pitch is seem incompetent. Other explore to fully understand levels of coaching/managing Who goes out to pitch? Who right field? Or who plays left coaches/managers process in every game. When a batter hits a ball, and a fielder reaches for it, the correct play depends on appropriate and precise decisions. The player must focus on the correct sequence in the decision process to field the ball first, secure it, then throws it to the appropriate person to complete the play.

In the decisions that are made, some have little effect on the game while others have consequences that are profoundly transforming. Our total lives are connected with decision-making. As soon as we open our eyes in the morning we begin to make decisions. We have to decide whether or not we get out of bed, or whether or not we stay in bed. Do we have or do we not have breakfast? What kind of clothing are we going to wear for the day? Do we make our beds or do we just leave it unkempt? Do we go to school today or do we not? How are we going to use our time today? What is our lifestyle going to be? What kinds of friends do we want to associate with? As one makes each decision, one needs to think about the consequences, because each decision can have a positive or negative impact on our lives.

Read the following life story and share with a peer what three significant lessons you have learned from the story.

Hank Aaron: The Decision Maker

One baseball player who personifies the most effective decision makers was Henry Louis Aaron - Hank Aaron. He would not allow anything to distract him from being one of baseball's most dominant homerun hitters. He was known at one time as baseball's all-time home-run king. He played 23 years as an outfielder for the Milwaukee Braves (which became the Atlanta Braves) and Milwaukee Brewers (1954–76). Aaron holds many of baseball's most distinguished records, including runs batted in (2,297), extra base hits (1,477), total bases (6,856) and most years with 30 or more home runs. He is also in the top five for career hits and runs. Aaron also had the record for most career home runs (755) until Barry Bonds broke it with his 756th home run on August 7, 2007, in San Francisco.

Aaron was born in a poor black section of Mobile, Alabama called "Down the Bay." He and his family moved to the middle class Toulminville neighborhood when he was a young boy. When he got to high school, Aaron played shortstop and third base on his school's team. Sensing his baseball skills, Aaron quit school in 1951 to play in the Negro Leagues for the Indianapolis Clowns

It wasn't a long stay. After leading his club to victory in the league's 1952 World Series, Aaron was recruited the following June to the Milwaukee Braves for $10,000. The Braves assigned their new player to one of their farm clubs, the Eau Claire Bears. Again Aaron did not disappoint anyone when he was named Northern League Rookie of the Year.

A year later, the 20-year-old Hank Aaron got his Major League start when a spring training injury to a Braves outfielder created a roster spot for him. Following a respectable first year, he hit .280 ERA. Aaron charged through the 1955 season with a blend of power (27 home runs), run production (106 runs batted in), and average (.328) that would come to define his long career. In 1956, after winning the first two batting titles, Aaron registered an unrivaled 1957 season, taking home the National League MVP and nearly nabbing the Triple Crown by hitting 44 home runs, knocking in another 132, and batting .322. That same year, Aaron demonstrated his ability to come up big when it counted most. His 11th inning homerun in late September propelled the Braves to the World Series, where he led the underdog Milwaukee to an upset win over the New York Yankees in seven games.

With the game still years away from the multi-million dollar contracts that would later dominate player salaries, Aaron's annual pay in 1959 was around $30,000. When he equaled that amount that same year in endorsements, Aaron realized there may be more in store for him if he continued to hit for power. "I noticed that they never had a show called 'Singles Derby,'" he said.

Aaron was right, of course, and over the next decade and a half, the always-fit Aaron banged out a steady stream of 30 and 40 homerun seasons. In 1973, at the age of 39, Aaron was still a force to reckon with, hitting a remarkable 40 homeruns to finish just one run behind Babe Ruth's all-time career mark of 714.

But the chase to beat the Babe's record revealed that the world of baseball was far from being free of the racial tensions that prevailed around it. As many as 3,000 letters a day poured into the Braves offices, for Aaron. Some wrote to congratulate him, but many others stated how they were appalled that a black man should break baseball's most sacred record. Death threats were a part of the mix. Of course, Aaron never allowed himself to be distracted by the threats. Instead he kept focused on his dream to play baseball and became one of the greatest hitters of all time. (With some modifications, the biography of Hank Aaron was taken from Wikipedia).

> *"High achievers spot rich opportunities swiftly, make big decisions quickly and move into action immediately. Follow these principles and you can make your dreams come true."* - *Robert H. Schuller*

ACTIVITY I

1. What is the significance of the quote in the box from Robert Schuller?

2. If you had to get to a large city from where you are at the moment, what plans would you make to get there?

   _____

3. If you would not take the most direct route to the city, what reason would you give for your choice?

   _____

4. Do you have trouble making decisions? Yes _____ No _____ Why?

5. In making decisions are you logical? _____ Impulsive? _____ or Vacillating? _____

6. In what ways can the list of ideas below impact your decisions?

   • Your beliefs

   • Your emotions

   • Your attitude

   • Your values

   • Your peers

The following ideas are critical in decision-making:

1. The importance of decisions must be established.

2. The purpose must be established in the decisions.

3. The criteria must be used in the decision.

4. The priorities must be maintained in the decision.

5. The alternatives must be thought of in decisions.

6. The consequences of decisions must be evaluated.

7. The troubles with decisions must be made known.

8. The timing of decisions are to be understood.

9. The knowledge that underlay decisions must be articulated. Jumping to conclusions often creates embarrassing conflicts.

10. The best decisions in life are in the correction stage -If you have made a bad decision, try to correct it quickly.

11. The best decisions in life are made with divine guidance. Seeking the help of God in your decisions is important. Do not pretend to be too wise.

> ➤ The Psalmist states, "*I will instruct you and teach you in the way you should go; I will counsel you and watch over you.*" Psalms 32:8

> ➤ Learn the impact of prayer on decisions – It helps us to focus on God's will.

> ➤ Learn how to listen to the Word – The Word of God has solid directions for every life.

> ➤ Learn to listen to Spiritual Counsel - Spiritual persons can be very helpful to us.

> ➤ Learn the power of the will in decision-making – The will is very powerful.

> ➤ Learn how to control your will: Your will needs to be properly controlled when you make   decisions.

Read the following short story titled "Muddy Road," credited to an anonymous author, then check the table that follows to show what the greatest contributor to the decision-making was.

Tanzan and Ekido were once traveling together down a muddy road. A heavy rain was still falling. Coming around a bend, they met a lovely girl in a silk kimono and sash, unable to cross the intersection. "Come on girl," said Tanzan at once. Lifting her in his arms, he carried her over the mud.

Ekido did not speak again until that night when they reached a lodging temple. Then he no longer could restrain himself. "We monks don't go near females," he told Tanzan, "especially not young and lovely ones. It is dangerous. Why did you do that?"

"I left the girl there," said Tanzan. "Are you still carrying her."

On the scale of 1-5 with 5 being the highest, check which idea has the greatest impact on your life	1	2	3	4	5
Leadership					
Resistance					
Conflict of interest					
Biases					
Lack of a common goal					
Lack of empathy					
Too much emotion					
Lack of willingness to change					

GOD'S MAP FOR DECISION MAKING

Joseph: An Effective Decision Maker

One of the greatest positive decision makers that one might ever encounter in history is Jacob's eleventh son- Joseph. Among his most critical decisions was one in his youthful life when he fled from the calculating and deceptive Mrs. Potiphar who tried to seduce him. The story, as it might be remembered, is that Joseph was sold into slavery by his brothers, and was taken to Egypt where Potiphar bought him as a household slave. Potiphar made Joseph the head of his household, but Potiphar's wife, struck by his manly, handsome appearance, tried to be intimate with him. Mrs. Potiphar became furious when Joseph resisted her advance and accused him falsely. She accused him of attempting to rape her and fled from her grasp leaving his coat in her hand, when she screamed. When Potiphar came home and heard his wife's story, he became terribly angry at Joseph and threw him into prison. After a while in the prison, (pit) Joseph came to

> *"Then he dreamed another dream and told it to his brothers and said, "Behold, I have dreamed another dream. Behold, the sun, the moon, and eleven stars were bowing down to me."*

the attention of Pharaoh because of his ability to interpret the dreams of Pharaoh's butler and baker. At thirty Joseph was promoted to become governor of Egypt, he also had to make several decisions including that of putting together a strategic plan for keeping the population of Egypt and the neighboring lands from starvation during seven years of famine.

What is clear about Joseph is that the small decisions that he made from his youth were most decisive. When he had to deal with the process of preparing Egypt for the famine, the reconciliation with his brothers, and the bringing of his family to Egypt, he was prepared and moved with precision...

Yes, the cumulative effect of small decisions can be great. A bad decision made over time can have rather serious effect. If a good decision is made, it leads to a great achievement. People who are ineffective at decision-making are also poor in their achievement. The life of Joseph truly reminds us that it is desirable to be effective decision-makers.

The way of indecision

Joel 3:14: *"Multitudes, multitudes in the valley of decision: for the day of the LORD is near in the valley of decision."*

Look at the Diamond below and reflect on your potential for effective Decisions

**WHAT IS THE RESULT OF
THE LATEST DECISION
YOU HAVE MADE?**

**PASS A VERDICT ON
YOUR LATEST CHOICE**

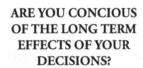

**ARE YOU CONCIOUS
OF THE LONG TERM
EFFECTS OF YOUR
DECISIONS?**

*Do you like what you have seen?
After you look back at the things you have seen concerning
your focus and management of your decisions, respond to the
questions on the next page that truly describe how effectively
you make decisions.*

TRANSFORMING YOUR ROAD MAP

1. Rate yourself on your capacity for making effective decisions.

   Excellent _____ Very good _____ Good _____ Poor _____ Very poor _____

2. What crucial skills do you think you need to be more effective in your decision making?

3. What are some major obstacles affecting your progress in decision-making process?

4. What are your areas of strengths with regards to making decisions?

5. What do you consider your weaknesses in making decisions?

6. What do you consider your best approach to making decisions?

7. If you face challenges in making decisions, what kinds of support do need to help you?

WORDS TO PONDER

Imagine yourself being a baseball player and in two appearances at the plate you hit two home runs. On your third appearance at the plate the pitcher tosses a ball that hits you on your forearm. You felt that what was done was rather vengeful. All kinds of negative thoughts are floating through your head at the moment, calling for a response. Think of how the following thought from American Entertainer Will Rogers would transform your response. "It's not what you pay a man, but what he costs you that counts."

Conclusion: This discussion is intended to help you with decision-making processes.

It is intended to help you make prejudgments on the steps you are to take.

It challenges you about indecisions

It helps you to avoid regrets

What have you learned about decision-making?

The way of indecision is hard

When we make a good decision, better choices are opened to us

DEDICATION

"Nobody trips over mountains. It is the small pebble that causes you to stumble. Pass all the pebbles in your path and you will find you have crossed the mountain."

- Anonymous

HOW DEDICATED ARE YOU?

To be an effective baseball player or any other such game one has to be totally dedicated. Just ask Big League player and they will tell you of the multiple years they have spent in Little League and Minor League or in some other training times they were frustrated and had continuing with their training. Ask week they have to pick up a bat early they have to get to training times they have to review the rules many times they have to go to the their muscles. What any successful players of any other game will tell you is that it takes dedication to be effective at their game.

There is no celebration without dedication

camps. Ask them how many to recommit themselves to them how many days each and a ball. Ask them how camp. Ask them how many of the game. Ask them how Gym to keep strengthening baseball player or successful

The dedicated baseball player knows what it means to stick around for a few extra swings, or get to the park early to catch a few extra ground balls. Such a player knows that one cannot skip practice and expect to be effective at the game. Playing through pain indicates the kind of commitment that is demanded. The point is, that anyone who wants to be an effective ball player (baseball or any other such game, in fact, any game) needs to know what it means to be dedicated; knows what it means to stick to a task.

Read the following life story and share with a peer what three significant lessons you have learned from the story.

Ken Griffey, Jr. - A Dedicated Man

Ken Griffey Jr. is one of Major League's premier baseball players. Faced by many setbacks with injuries, Griffey's dedication to the game sets him apart as one of the most prolific home run hitters and best defensive players in the history of baseball. He is fifth on the list of most career home runs, and is tied for the record of most consecutive games with home runs. He has won 10 gold glove awards. His name is not publicized as some of the other great stars of baseball, because he played for the Seattle Mariners, Cincinnati Reds, and Chicago White Sox - teams with less media exposure than the Yankees, Red Sox and Dodgers. However, he is respected among the greats of baseball players.

Griffey was born in Donora, Pennsylvania, the same area as the Hall of Famer Stan Musial. Griffey's family moved to Cincinnati, Ohio when his father Ken Griffey Sr. was invited to play for the Cincinnati Reds. Ken was in the clubhouse during his father's back-to-back championships in the 1975 and 1976 World Series. He attended Archbishop Moeller High School, where he was the baseball player of the year in 1986 and 1987. He also played football for three years. In 1987, Griffey was selected with the first overall pick of that year's amateur draft by the Seattle Mariners. In his eleven seasons with Seattle (1989 to 1999) Griffey established himself as one of the most prolific and exciting players of the era, racking up 2,763 hits, 630 home runs, 1,821 RBIs, and 184 stolen bases. He led the American League in home runs four seasons (1994, 1997, 1998, 1999), and was voted the A.L. MVP in 1997, and maintained a .299 batting average. What is admirable about Ken Griffey, Jr. was his uncomplaining spirit and dedication, even in times of injuries. (With some modifications, the biography of Ken Griffey Jr. was taken from Wikipedia).

> *Life will always throw you curves, just keep fouling them off... the right pitch will come, but when it does, be prepared to run the bases. - Rick Maksian*

ACTIVTY I

Explain

1. What do you understand by Rice Maksian's words?

_____

_____

2. How can being dedicated to a task lead to success or failure?

_____

_____

3. Describe the relationship between dedication and dreaming.

_____

_____

Name any two things in life to which you are so wholeheartedly committed that you would not trade them for anything.

(1)_____ (2)_____

ACTIVTY II –Just Share

Instruction: With a colleague take a position on the following statements or arguments   then be prepared to share your answers with your whole group.

1. There is no relationship between dedication and personal sacrifices.

_____

_____

2. One cannot achieve his/her goals without some kind of social network of friends/relatives.

_____

_____

3. One cannot be effective without some fundamental sense of values.

ACTIVTY III

Think of someone you admire because of their commitment to building some specific skills that made them a success story, then share that story with a colleague.

For example, tell of a person who has faced tough times, or had some personal issues but was able beat the odds because of being dedicated to being successful. Tell some challenges that person had to fight.

a. _____ b. _____

c. _____ d. _____

Describe with your group how you feel concerning the following sayings of the wise.

1. "Don't aim at success - the more you aim at it and make it a target, the more you are going to miss it. For success, like happiness, cannot be pursued; it must ensue...as the unintended side-effect of one's personal dedication to a course greater than oneself." -Victor Frankl

2. "A champion is someone who gets up, even when he can't." -Jack Dempsey

3. "Confidence is the result of hours and days and weeks and years of constant work and dedication." -Roger Staubach

4. "Almost always, the creative dedicated minority has made the world better." -Martin Luther King Jr.

5. "No steam or gas drives anything until it is confined. No life ever grows great until it is focused, dedicated, disciplined." -Harry Fosdick

6. "There is no chance, no destiny, no fate, that can hinder or control the firm resolve of a determined soul." - Ella Wheeler Wilcox

7. "Your subconscious conditioning determines your thinking. Your thinking determines your decisions. Your decisions determine your actions, which eventually determine your outcomes." – T. Harve Eker

GOD'S MAP FOR YOUR PERSONAL SPIRITUAL DEDICATION

Joseph: A True Example of Dedication

Potiphar must have noticed something special about Joseph's dedication when he placed him in the position of superintendent of his house. He must have watched to see how well Joseph fixed his mind on his dream. He must have perceived that Joseph was a young man who was steadfast to principles. He must have noted his dedication to the vision of being honest to God. He must have seen his desire to remain pure. He must have observed that Joseph was devoted wholly and earnestly to the specific goals of life. Joseph is a true example of what dedication means.

One can understand the shock on Potiphar's face when his wife reported to him the news that Joseph tried to rape her. A seed of doubt might have likely entered Potiphar's mind. But Potiphar did not pause so long to think about it. It was his wife, and he had to do something about it, therefore he quickly placed Joseph in prison. Of course, prison did not change the dedication of Joseph. While in prison his dedication led him to be seen by the baker and the butler. When they had their troubling dreams they went to him for consultation and support, which he gave them by interpreting their dreams. After his release from prison, and promotion to governorship he was able to demonstrate in a public way, what dedication meant. Yes, a point that must be made before

> *"Look, the dreamer comes, come let us kill him."*

the end of our brief reflection is that in reality, dedication has to do with our private commitments more than our public actions. Ceremonies of dedication might be held for a baby, or to mark specific transitions in a person's life, but the true significance of such dedication cannot be known until one observes the attitudes and actions that follow the ceremony of dedication. Does such a person then, understand that his/her time and life are purposed to a specific function? The point is that, true dedication does not depend so much upon external stimulation as much as it depends upon our private commitments and motivations. The one who truly understands this will know then why the life of Joseph had no place for compromise.

Here are some instructions that will help one to understand the import of dedication.

1. **Taking good advice**

   Proverbs 23:12 (NIV) *"Apply your heart to instruction and your ears to words of knowledge."*

2. **Making you commitment**

   Proverbs 16:3 (NIV) *"Commit to the Lord whatever you do, and your plans will succeed."*

Look at the Diamond below and ask yourself how dedicated you are:

YOUR WILLINGNESS TO
STAY ON BASE

CHECK YOUR LOYALTY

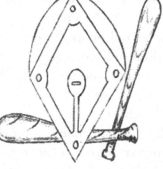

YOUR COMMITMENTS TO
THE JOB

Do you like what you have seen?
After you look back at the things you have seen
concerning your focus and management of your life,
respond to the questions on the next page that truly
describe your level of dedication.

TRANSFORMING YOUR ROAD MAP

1. Rate yourself at the moment, in your attitude to dedication.

   Very dedicated _____ Average _____ Low dedication _____ Not dedicated _____

2. Where would you like to go from where you are regarding your spirit of dedication?

3. Do you see any obstacle affecting your spirit of dedication? If you do, tell which is the greatest.

4. List three things that could prevent you from being very dedicated.

   a. _____ b. _____ c. _____

5. What do you consider could be your weakest point in the area of dedication?

6. What kind of things do you need to do in order to meet the challenges of total dedication?

"The person who makes a success of living is the one who sees his goal steadily and aims for it unswervingly. That is dedication. "

- Cecil B. De Mille

WORDS TO PONDER

Imagine yourself as a baseball catcher and a game is to be played in which you were not scheduled to catch. In the last few weeks you have caught 30 games without a break and you really feel exhausted. The night of the game the team's manager says the scheduled catcher is not feeling well and the other catcher on the team has just arrived from the Minors. The manager insists that the only available catcher is you. Think of how the following thought might affect your sense of commitment.

"Use your very life as fuel, and trust that while the fire in your heart is transforming your experience, the heat and warmth you are producing will be attracting new opportunities to you beyond your wildest dreams." – Carol Orsborn

Conclusion: This discussion is to help you clarify your highest levels of life commitments.

We reference the questions of commitment under the topic of dedication

Being dedicated is essential for success in anything.

Being dedicated means accepting the pain of discipline. (Are you willing to make the sacrifice?)

Dedication demands time, effort, and consistency. (Are you willing to pay the price of dedication?)

"The price of success is hard work, dedication to the job at hand, and the determination that whether we win or lose, we have applied the best of ourselves to the task at hand."

— *Vince Lombardi*

HOW PERSISTENT ARE YOU?

One might have all the ability in the world, but if such a one lacks determination, such a person will not be successful at baseball or any other game, profession, or career. When scouts look for good ball players, they not only seek talent and ability but they watch closely to see if the player is persistent in practice, as well as how well that person can deal with frustrations.

Ask any baseball player or players of other games or anyone involved in the game of life, how do they feel when they have set forth to reach a goal and along the way they find that they become frustrated. Ask them whether they feel a sense of irritability, anger, loss of confidence, loss of energy, or loss of enthusiasm and happiness. Ask them how such feelings affect their performance. We are profoundly intrigued when we watch ball players or other persons who get stuck in their frustration for a long time, how their performance goes in a downward spiral. Until they are able to get a new mental attitude which states that their present failure is not the end of their road, they generally perform very poorly.

People who have a determined will are able to pick themselves up after their brief moment of frustration, while others get stuck in their negative condition for a long time. Those who overcome their frustration know that they must use resources from within and outside of themselves. They will have to take encouragement where it exists and must turn away from negative mental images where such exists. The determined person cannot allow external circumstances to control them. They cannot be ruled by failure. A person of determination will have to exercise patience and courage. They must learn how to wait through times of frustration and keep pushing ahead no matter what.

Read the following life story and share with a peer what three significant lessons you have learned from the story.

James Abbott- A Man of Determination

Maybe you have heard about James Anthony Abbott, the baseball player who was born without a right hand. He was born in Flint, Michigan and attended Flint Central High School where he demonstrated his talents as a stand-out pitcher and quarterback. He played ball for the Grossi Baseball Club in the Connie Mack Leagues of Michigan. In 1985, he was drafted in the 36th round by the Toronto Blue Jays, but did not sign. Instead, he moved on to the University of Michigan. From 1985 to 1988 he played under Coach Bud Middaugh, leading his team to two Big Ten championships. In 1987, he won the James E. Sullivan Award as the top amateur athlete in the United States, becoming the first baseball pitcher to win the award. He was the flag-bearer for the United States at the 1987 Pan American Games in Indianapolis, and helped to lead the USA to a first place finish. The highlight of his amateur career came when he pitched the final game in the 1988 Summer Olympics, winning a gold medal for the United States. He was voted the Big Ten Athlete of the Year in 1988. He was selected 8th overall by the California Angels in the 1988 draft, and from 1989 to 1999 played a career of ten seasons for the California Angels, the New York Yankees, the Chicago White Sox, and the Milwaukee Brewers. Currently, he is a motivational speaker across the United States. Speak about determination; Abbot has it. (With some modifications, the biography of James Abbott was taken from Wikipedia).

> *"Every day is a new opportunity. You can build on yesterday's success or put its failures behind and start over again. That's the way life is, with a new game every day, and that's the way baseball is." - Bob Feller*

ACTIVTY I

How does the following story enhance your understanding of determination?

In ancient times, a king had a boulder placed on a certain roadway, and then he hid himself and watched to see if anyone would remove the huge rock. Some of the king's wealthiest merchants and courtiers came by and simply walked around it. Many loudly blamed the King for not keeping the roads clear, but they did nothing about getting the stone out of the way.

Later a peasant came along carrying a load of vegetables. Upon approaching the boulder, the peasant laid down his burden and tried to move the stone to the side of the road. After much pushing and straining, he finally succeeded. The peasant had just picked up his load of vegetables, when he noticed a purse lying in the road where the boulder had been. The purse contained many gold coins and a note from the king indicating that the gold was for the person who removed the boulder from the roadway. The peasant learned what many of us never understand!

Think of a movie that you have seen or a book you have read that showed determination. Comment on how an attitude of determination was displayed.

_____

_____

Name two obstacles that you have faced and believe you confronted in a positive way.

1. _____

2. _____

ACTIVTY II

_____

How might an attitude of procrastination impact a person's capacity to succeed?

_____

Evaluate the following sayings of the wise and share with your group what you think is meant.

1. "Procrastination is the art of keeping up with yesterday."
   - Don Marquis

2. "Only Robinson Crusoe had everything done by Friday."
   - Author Unknown

3. "Every duty which is bidden to wait returns with seven fresh duties at its back."
   -Charles Kingsley

4. "Until you value yourself, you will not value your time. Until you value your time, you will not do anything with it."
   - M. Scott Peck

5. "Nothing is so fatiguing as the eternal hanging on of an uncompleted task."
   -William James

6. "Be wise today; 'tis madness to defer. Next day the fatal precedent will plead; thus on, til wisdom is pushed out of life."
   - Edward Young

7. "If you want to make an easy job seem mighty hard, just keep putting off doing it."
   - Olin Miller

What do you think of the following suggestions to overcome procrastination?

1.) **Persuade yourself** – Most procrastination is the result of irrational thinking. Irrational thinking often leads to "awful rising". You talk yourself to procrastinate by putting off the task not because it is simply unpleasant, but because you think it is awful. It is horrible. Of course, none of these descriptions are really accurate. Convince yourself instead that this is worth doing, even if it is hard getting started. Tell yourself I may not enjoy paperwork but I can certainly do it, and I might feel good when it is done. So persuade yourself.

2.) Challenge yourself – Don't put off things that you need to do – For example, if you generally excuse yourself by saying "I work very well under pressure," argue that pressure rushes you and does not give you time you need to be creative.

3.) How much time do you spend on unscheduled activities each day?

4.) How much time do you spend before the TV or on video games or the telephone or other time consuming gadgets each day?

_____

Now reflect on how you use time by answering yes or no to the following.

Do you schedule time? _____

Do you waste time? _____

Do you prioritize time? _____

Do you have too much to do in too little time? _____

Do you have time for family? _____

Do you spend too much time with friends? _____

Do spend too much time with TV and Phones, Video games, etc? _____

Do you have a set time for going to bed **at nights** and a set time to rise **in the mornings**? _____

Do you have enough time for your school work and your jobs? _____

Do you have a planned free time? _____

Are you comfortable with how you were able to answer the questions above?

_____

If you are not satisfied, what would you like to change?

_____

GOD'S MAP FOR PERSONAL SPIRITUAL DETERMINATION

Joseph: A Man of Determination

Only a few individuals can match the "doggedness" of Joseph. Even though his brothers hated him so much that they sold him into Egyptian slavery, there was a quality in his character that motivated him. Such a quality was made most evident when Mrs. Potiphar sought to seduce him. She tried to become intimate with him, but he resisted her on several occasions. He was determined that he would not defile his body, nor displease his God. He would not be unfair to his master and disrespect his wife by acquiescing to her advances. His determination led him to run from the seductress, even leaving his coat in her hand as she tried to trap him. Mrs. Potiphar, sensing that her little trick failed, accused Joseph falsely and had him thrown into jail. Going to jail for a crime he did not commit, would have been enough to break the will of Joseph. However, he did not despair. His courageous attitude, and stamina, endeared him to the jail officials and several inmates. His attitude allowed him to survive the ordeal. He was promoted to the governorship of Egypt, through a series of events. He made connection with his brothers, and his determination allowed him to persist until he was reunited with the whole family in Egypt. He was also determined to ensure that his brothers were changed men. Joseph was not easily frustrated. He knew what he wanted and used various strategies to achieve it. Joseph was not determined to do just as he pleased, but instead he acted on principle, always wanting to do what was right and to go forward. The reality is that without determination there is no forward movement in a life.

Reflect on the admonitions below and let them guide you in your quest for success.

1. **Determined to hold on to instruction**

   Proverbs 4:13-15; 20-22: "Hold on to instruction, do not let it go; and it will be well, for it is your life. Do not set foot on the path of the wicked or walk in the way of evil men. Avoid it, do not travel on it; turn from it and go on your way. My son, pay attention to what I say; listen closely to my words. Do not let them out of your sight, keep them within your heart; for they are life to those who find them and health to a man's whole body."

2. **Guarding the teaching**

   Proverbs 7:2, 3: "Keep my commands and you will live; guard my teachings as the apple of your eye. Bind them on your fingers; write them on the tablet of your heart."

3. **Living through times of trouble**

   Proverbs 24:10 - If you falter in times of trouble, how small is your strength!

Look at the Diamond Below to Test Your Determination

RESOLUTION TO PERSEVERE AT ALL COSTS

DOGGEDNESS TO WIN

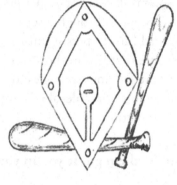

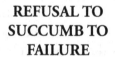

REFUSAL TO SUCCUMB TO FAILURE

Do you like what you have seen?
After you look back at the things you have seen concerning your focus and management of your determination, respond to the questions on the next page that truly describe your doggedness.

TRANSFORMING YOUR ROAD MAP

1. Rate yourself on your level of determination to succeed

    High-level _____   Average _____   Low-level _____   None _____

2. Where do you expect such determination to take you?

    _____

3. What do you see as the greatest obstacle that could affect your determination to succeed?

    _____

4. When you think about your level of determination, what are some strengths you have that can help you?

    _____

5. What are some negative issues you see that could impair your determination toward success?

    _____

6. If you believe that you have challenges regarding your determination, list them.

    _____

"An ant on the move does more than a dozing ox. "

- Lao Tzu

WORDS TO PONDER

Don't quit

When things go wrong, as they sometimes will,
When the road you're trudging seems all uphill,
When the funds are low and the debts are high,
And you want to smile, but you have to sigh,
When care is pressing you down a bit,
Rest, if you must, but don't you quit.

Life is queer with its twists and turns,
As every one of us sometimes learns,
And many a failure turns about,
When he might have won had he stuck it out;
Don't give up though the pace seems slow--
You may succeed with another blow.

Often the goal is nearer than,
It seems to a faint and faltering man,
Often the struggler has given up,
When he might have captured the victor's cup,
And he learned too late when the night slipped down,
How close he was to the golden crown.

Success is failure turned inside out--
The silver tint of the clouds of doubt,
And you never can tell how close you are,
It may be near when it seems so far,
So stick to the fight when you're hardest hit--
It's when things seem worst that you must not quit.

- Author unknown

DOING

"Knowing is not enough; we must apply. Being willing is not enough; we must do."

– Leonardo Da Vinci

WHAT IS YOUR WORK ATTITUDE LIKE?

It is said that one might have ambition and ability, with a negative attitude and no action and be a guaranteed failure. In effect, a actions are keys to one's successes. great baseball player. One can is sold on the market. One can One might be good at talking a might buy all the baseball cards in multiple baseball games. One

> *There is no celebration without action*
> *-Doing*

good attitude and effective One can dream of being a buy every baseball book that study all the rules of baseball. good game of baseball. One the world. One might attend might know every baseball

trade. However one will never be a baseball player if one never plays baseball. Moreover, one will never be a top class ball player, if one practices. Yes, persistent practice is the key to developing mastery in whatever truly matters to a person. if one never practices to play the game. To play baseball one's dream must spring into action. Successful baseball players know their **ambitions**, **abilities**, and **attitudes** are only effective if they are acted on (DOING).

Read the following life story and share with a peer what three significant lessons you have learned from the story.

Derek Jeter – The Doer

Derek Sanderson Jeter is an all American professional baseball player. He has been playing shortstop for the New York Yankees since his major league debut. He has also served as the Yankees' team captain since 2003. Derek entered the Major Leagues in 1995, and the following year he won the Rookie of the Year Award, and helped the Yankees win the 1996 World Series. Jeter was also a member of the championship-winning teams in 1998, 1999, 2000, and 2009. In 2000, Jeter became the only player to win both the All-Star Game MVP Award and the World Series MVP Award in the same year. He was selected as an All-Star ten times, and has won the Silver Slugger and Gold Glove awards on four occasions and is regarded as the consummate professional by teammates and opponents alike. He has earned a reputation as being a very reliable contributor in the postseason.

Jeter was born at Chilton Memorial Hospital in Pequannock Township, New Jersey in 1974. His father, Dr. Sanderson Charles Jeter, a substance abuse counselor is an African American and his mother, Dorothy, is Caucasian of Irish/German descent. His father played shortstop at Fisk University in Tennessee. Of course, what is most notable about Derrick Jeter is his discipline and dedication to hard work. He became the captain of the Yankees very early in his playing career because he was a model of hard work, and it was noted that he could become an effective mentor for his team mates. He is always well respected on and off the field, and remains one of the few remaining icons of baseball who is not named for any contemptible activities. T. Harve Eker says, "Thoughts lead to feelings. Feelings lead to actions. Actions lead to results." One can say, Derrick Jeter knows how to act. (With some modifications, the biography of Derek Jeter was taken from Wikipedia).

> *"If you're not practicing, somebody else is, somewhere, and he'll be ready to take your job."*
>
> *- Brooks Robinson*

ACTIVITY I

1. Are you the kind of person who likes to (a) take action or (b) the kind who only thinks and talks? _____ Explain your answer. _____
_____
_____

2. Name two things that you do really well? _____

   a.) _____

   b.) _____

3. Name one thing that you wish you could do better _____

   a.) _____

   b.) _____

4. What are the things that other people think you do really well? _____

5. What is your greatest passion in life? _____

6. What do you enjoy doing well? _____

7. Areyouthekindofpersonwhofindsopportunitiestodowhatyouthinkneedstobedone,ordoyouwaitforsomeone to point out what you need to do? _____

   Explain _____

8. Choose which of the following would best describe who you really are. Check at least two.

   An observer _____

   An activist _____

   A spectator _____

   A participant _____

   An analyst _____

   A bummer _____ (Just eat hamburgers, watch TV late at nights, sleep late next morning, ride the waves, smoke pot, and let your parents take care of business or what.)

   A procrastinator _____

9. From the things you checked off above tell what you wish could be different.

   _____

   _____

ACTIVITY II

Discuss with a friend what you think of the following statements.

"Actions speak louder than words."

"Nothing will come your way unless you take some action." T. Harve Eker

"Where attention goes energy flows." – T. Harve Eker

"What you are doing is where you are going." – Dr. Sylvan Lashley

"The firefly only gives off light when it is flying." – Gloria Gaithar

"He who tills his land will be satisfied with bread, but he who follows frivolity is devoid of understanding." - Proverbs 12:11, Bible

"If you only do what you know you can do – you never do very much." - Tom Krause.

"He who loves his life will lose it, and he who hates his life in in this word shall keep it into eternal life" – Jesus (John 12:25).

"Whatever your hand finds to do, do it with all your might, for in the grave, where you are going, there is neither working nor planning nor knowledge nor wisdom." – Ecclesiastes 9:10.

ACTIVITY III

A. Hyperactivity:

1. Hyperactivity is the condition of being hyperactive. Do you understand what is meant by hyperactivity?

2. How might hyper-activity lead to self-absorption or distractions?

3. What are the dangers of rushing into activities before you think them through?

4. What are the benefits of thinking through your actions before engaging in them?

B. Purposeful activity:

1. How is purposeful activity different from hyperactivity? _____

2. What do you think of the following comment by T. Harve Eker? *"Purposeful activity focuses on results."*- _____

3. Evaluate the following stanzas from Henry Wadsworth Longfellow's *Psalm of Life,* in light of how you see your life of activity at the present moment.

Lives of great men all remind us
We can make our lives sublime,
And, departing, leave behind us
Footprints on the sands of time;

Footprints, that perhaps another,
Sailing o'er life's solemn main,
A forlorn and shipwrecked brother,
Seeing, shall take heart again.

Let us, then, be up and doing,
With a heart for any fate;
Still achieving, still pursuing,
Learn to labor and to wait.

_____

_____

_____

_____

C. It has been said that people are creatures of habit. If you agree with such a view make a list of the habits that you want to break in order to construct a more purposeful life.

1. _____

2. _____

3. _____

4. _____

D. Most persons find it difficult to break bad habits; however, it is quite possible if one is prepared to follow certain steps. Psychologists have often suggested the following keys to transforming your habits.

1. Identify the triggers for your bad habit.

2. Rather than simply trying to rid yourself of a bad habit, replace the bad habit with a good habit.

3. Consistently focus on the changes you are trying to make.

4. Learn to avoid those situations that encourage your bad habit.

5. Acknowledge that the greatest tendency of humanity is to focus on the negative. Stay positive.

6. Ask for help to transform your habit. – Read a book *The Power of Habit* and share with a friend what you have learned.

7. If you fail in your effort to transform your habits, do not give up; try, try, try again.

GOD'S MAP FOR EFFECTICE ACTIONS

Joseph: A Man of Action

Many interpreters believe that what brought Joseph to be the overseer and guardian of Potiphar's house was that Potiphar saw in Joseph a young man of action. These interpreters think that what is meant by "That the Eternal was with him and all that he had he gave into his hand, save the bread which he ate." (Genesis 39:3-6fp), shows that Potipher saw Joseph as one who was responsible and accountable for his actions. The comment at the end of chapter 39:6, "And Joseph was handsome and good looking" was meant to introduce the reader to something different, specifically, the seductive attempt of Lady Potiphar. In effect, Joseph was not made the steward or overseer of Potiphar's house because he was handsome, but because he was a person who demonstrated a positive attitude in doing work. In his early years when his dad sent him on a long journey to visit with his brothers, he did not grumble, but went. When he was sold into slavery, he evidently showed himself to be responsible at the tasks he was given to do. Such an attitude led to his becoming the chief steward of Potiphar's house. Later when he was put into the "pit" he once again demonstrated how responsible he was, even though he was young. His positive attitude helped him to be promoted as overseer, not just of the king's court, but of the whole land of Egypt.

> *When his master saw that the LORD was with him and that the LORD gave him success in everything he did, Joseph found favor in his eyes and became his attendant.*

Below are biblical pointers on how to develop diligence. Read them and see how they impact you.

The reward of diligence

Proverbs 22:29 (NIV): Do you see a man skilled in his work? He will serve before kings; he will not serve before obscure men.

Proverbs 6:6-8 (NIV): Go to the ant, you sluggard; consider its ways and be wise! It has no commander, no overseer or ruler, yet it stores its provisions in summer and gathers its food at harvest.

Look at the Diamond below to test your capacity for positive activity

**WORKING
EFFECTIVELY AT
FULFILLING YOUR
DUTY**

**TAKING INITIATIVE
IN WHATEVER YOU
DO**

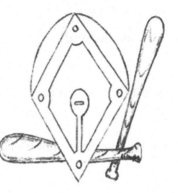

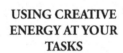

**USING CREATIVE
ENERGY AT YOUR
TASKS**

*Do you like what you have seen?
After you look back at the things you have seen concerning
you're the management of your actions, respond to the
questions on the next page that truly describe who you are
in attitude and actions.*

TRANSFORMING YOUR ROAD MAP

1. Do you see yourself as a person of purpose? Give your response, by beginning two sentences with the word **Because**.

2. Where would you want your actions to take you?

3. What could be the greatest obstacle affecting your progress toward being an effective person?

4. What skill sets do you have that set you apart as a doer? List them.

5. What do you see as a weakness that could affect your progress in becoming effective *"doer"*?

6. What kind of help do you need to correct the challenges you face in becoming a *"doer"*?

Conclusion: The point of this discussion is to help you formulate a strategy for action.

It is said a person must learn to *"act or be acted upon."*

Actions are the means through which we transform our aspirations.

When people make promises about things, they need to learn how to carry them out. Are you an actor or a promise?

DARING

"When the decks are stacked against you, you have to have guts."

-D. Robert Kennedy

LEARNING TO TAKE RISKS

In baseball games, one of the most fascinating aspects to watch is the sequence of pitches a pitcher seeks to throw. When a batter, who hardly ever strikes out, is standing in the batting box and the pitch count is three balls and no strikes, or three balls and two strikes, what does a pitcher do, especially if two batters are on first and second or second and third base? It is always very important to watch pitchers at this stage as they make fundamental decisions as to what pitches they are going to throw next. Will the pitcher get fearful and throw the ball away? Will the pitcher throw a strike or just hide the ball? Will the pitcher dare? Does the pitcher have the personal self-assurance to dare? Or is the pitcher filled with fear? Whether in pitching or in running the bases, in batting or fielding, the thing that allows a team to win more games than others is the team members' ability to dare – to take a risk, to set up a challenge.

There is no celebration without positive daring or risk taking

Read the following life story and share with a peer what three significant lessons you have learned from the story.

Nolan Ryan- The Risk Taker

During his career Nolan Ryan was one of Major League Baseball's most daring pitchers. He would throw the ball to the plate over 100 miles per hour and dare any batter to hit it. Even when he was over the age of 40, he was still throwing pitches over 100 miles per hour. He played for 27 years and had 526 wins. His 5,714 career strikeouts rank first in baseball history. Ryan was an eight-time MLB All-Star. He compiled 53 MLB records with seven no-hitters during his career. He holds the Guinness Book of World Records for throwing the fastest baseball pitched at 100.9 miles per hour. Rockwell scientists recorded it on August 20, 1974 against Bee Bee Richard of the Chicago White Sox on a 3-2 high fastball in the 9th inning. The ball crossed home plate in 0.38 seconds. The nickname "the Ryan Express" had its origin with the New York media. While with the Mets, the movie "Von Ryan's Express" became a big hit.

Ryan was born in Refugio, Texas in 1947 in a family of six. As a child, he threw objects at every target he could find. His dad was fascinated with his aptitude to throw and encouraged him to play baseball. Soon after graduating high school, he was drafted by the New York Mets where he became the youngest player then, in Major League history. He was later traded to the California Angels where he spent seven seasons. He moved on to the Houston Astros and then the Texas Rangers where he made history with his 300th win. He is currently the owner of the Texas Rangers. One of the greatest things to be remembered about Nolan Ryan is that he never backed down from pitching his fast balls no matter who was in the batters' box. He had a lot of personal confidence and was ever determined to win. (With some modifications, the biography of Nolan Ryan was taken from Wikipedia).

> *"I became a good pitcher when I stopped trying to make them miss the ball and started trying to make them hit it."*
>
> -Sandy Koufax

ACTIVTY I

Risk is part of the journey to optimal performance or failure. Discuss with a friend the following:

1. Which of the following qualities of character people who are great baseball pitchers must have?

    a. Temerity

    b. Timidity

    c. Tough-mindedness

    d. Trepidation

2. What is the relationship between a great vision for winning and risk taking?

3. How useful is great ability without risk taking?

4. Name three qualities of an effective risk taker?

    a. _____ b. _____ c. _____

5. What values are to be placed on adaptability and humility in risk taking?

6. What kinds of risks are you willing to take that will provide you with positive steps to where you want to go in life? _____

7. Have you ever felt that your fear of risking taking has affected or will affect:

    a. Your possibility for a great discovery? Yes_____ No_____

    b. Your ability to converse with others? Yes_____ No_____

    c. Your success in finding good relationships? Yes_____ No_____

    d. Your ability to learn a new language? Yes_____ No_____

    e. Your understanding of a particular technology? Yes_____ No_____

    f. Your search for a job? Yes_____ No_____

8. Name a behavior in which any friend of yours has engaged that you would say was risky, but not reckless.

9. How much sacrifice are you willing to make for what you want to accomplish in the next two years?

10. How might one's risky decisions impact those around him/her?

ACTIVTY II

On a scale of 1-5 with 1 being lowest and 5 being the highest, check yourself on the following risk -taking characteristics

    1. Courageous _____

    2. Cautious _____

    3. Adventurous _____

    4. Fearful _____

    5. Audacious _____

    6. Timid _____

    7. Brave _____

    8. Cowardly _____

    9. Propensity towards self-injury _____

How comfortable are you with the risk of change? _____

How much are you challenged by losses? _____

Are you the kind of person that always feels better when you walk on eggshells or on rocks? Why is this so? _____

All of life assumes elements of risk, are you ready to be a risk taker? _____

Check which of the following characteristics are most needful in your life, then comment in a side bar what you wish you could get rid of.Giftedness _____

    1. Respectfulness _____

    2. Self-Confidence _____

    3. Indecisiveness _____

    4. Selfishness _____

    5. Weak-willed _____

    6. Undependable _____

    7. Egotistical _____

    8. Strong-willed _____

    9. Determination _____

   10. Loudness _____

   11. Self-centeredness _____

   12. Consistency _____

   13. Combativeness _____

   14. Negligence _____

   15. Aggressiveness _____

   16. Rudeness _____

What do you think about the following sayings of the Wise?

1. "If you don't want it bad enough to risk losing it – you don't want it bad enough."
   — Tom Krause.

2. "It is not because things are difficult that we do not dare; it is because we do not dare that they are difficult." - Seneca

3. "Those who dare to fail miserably can achieve greatly." – Robert D. Kennedy

4. "It is impossible to win the race unless you venture to run, impossible to win the victory unless you dare to battle." - Richard M. Demos

5. "We have to dare to be ourselves, however frightening or strange that self may prove to be." May Sarton

6. "Most people live and die with their music still unplayed. They never dare to try." - Mary Kay Ash

7. "Who dares nothing, need hope for nothing." - Johann Friedrich Von Schiller

8. "If you have never dared, you have not lived." – S. June Kennedy

BE CAREFUL WHAT YOU CALL IMPOSSIBLE – BECAUSE AS SOON AS YOU CALL SOMETHING IMPOSSIBLE, YOU MAKE IT SO – QUOTED BY JOHN EDMOND HAGGAI

GOD'S PLAN FOR MAKING A DARE

Joseph: The Risk Taker

He dared to dream and tell his dreams. This is what Joseph did. He had his dreams and dared to tell them to his brothers and his father. He might not have suspected the cost of telling, or did he? It is often a dare to dream and share the dream. Harriet Tubman said, "Every great dream begins with a dreamer." Oscar Wilde said, "A dreamer is one who can only find his way by moonlight, and his punishment is that he sees the dawn before the rest of the world." Yes, when one dreams one is entering risky territory, for such a one is going outside of what is normal for ordinary human beings. Joseph not only took a dare when he dreamed and shared it, but when he interpreted the dream of the baker and butler, and later, the dream of Pharaoh, he dared. He did not know, in each case, the total outcome, but he stated what God had told him. A profound reality is that when one speaks one dares. Of course, some kinds of speeches are most daring, like when one has to stand up for truth. To speak falsehood does not take much daring, except the fear that one will be found out. But people who speak lies pack one lie upon another to cover up the deceit. Our life's journey is filled with dares, and only as one dares to dare that one will find one's dream coming to fruition.

Of course, not every dare is positive. For example, when Mrs. Potiphar challenged Joseph to a sexual dare, he refused because he understood the negative consequences of such a behavior. Risky behaviors such as those connected with substance abuse, violence, promiscuous sexual activities,

> *And though she spoke to Joseph day after day, he refused to go to bed with her or even be with her.*

and other forms of carefree living, are known to affect human beings in all stages of development. The negative effects are often seen in physical, intellectual and relational conditions; however there are many other kinds of effects. The point is that if Joseph had participated in risky behaviors he likely would never have become one of the most effective governors of Egypt. The annals of history are littered with lives that could have been otherwise profoundly great, but that they allowed their risky behaviors to destroy them.

Allow the following biblical quotations to guide you as you seek to dare:

1. Excuses we present to God

Proverbs 26:13-14 *"The slothful man saith, There is a lion in the way; a lion is in the streets. As the door turneth upon his hinges, so doth the slothful upon his bed."* KJV

2. The value of good friends

Proverbs 18:24 *"A person who has friends must show them self friendly: and there is a friend that sticks closer than a brother."*

On the Diamond, look at yourself to see what is your capacity for risk taking

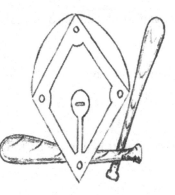

DO YOU FALL APART AT THE SEAMS WHEN YOU HAVE TO DO ANYTHING?

ARE YOU COMFORTABLE TAKING RISKS?

THE MORE CHANCES YOU TAKE THE BETTER THE POSSIBILITIES OF SUCCESS

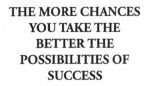

Do you like what you have seen?
After you look back at the things you have seen concerning your capacity for daring, respond to the questions on the next page that truly describe your level of tolerance for risk- taking.

TRANSFORMING YOUR ROAD MAP

1. Are you a very fearful person? Rate yourself on the fear factor at the moment.

   Very fearful _____ Some-what fearful _____ Not fearful _____

2. If you have fears, how much do you think you need to deal with them? Why or why not?

3. Name any level of success that you might have achieved by now if your fears had not been driving you?

4. Do you have any appetite for risk taking? Name your strongest or weakest areas.

5. Are you a person who focuses on the mistakes that you might make before taking risks?

6. What kinds of support do you need to correct the challenges you face in the area of risk taking?

"There are risks and costs to a program of action. But they are far less than the long-range risks and costs of comfortable inaction."

-John F. Kennedy

Conclusion: The point of this discussion is to challenge you to take risks.

Every success story involves people who have taken risks.

Are you a risk taker? Are you ready to take another risk?

"Discipline is the refining fire by which talent becomes ability."

- Roy Smith

LEARNING TO DEAL WITH LIFE'S FAILURE

If one does not learn the significance of the statement above from Roy Smith in any other context of life, it is clear that one sure will in baseball. It is said, "Baseball is the most maturing game among games, with the exception of fishing." Baseball players or their fans just never dream a perfect game or season. Few pitchers ever pitch a "perfect" game. No team in baseball ever played a perfect season. All players know what it means to have a bad day. All players, who understand the game, have learned to accept losses.

> *There is no celebration without Discipline*

Although personal discipline might not always determine a win in every baseball game, yet it is understood that those persons or teams that are consistent winners, are the teams with the most disciplined players.

It is not just those persons who have the greatest ability that win, but those who have disciplined or trained themselves. Some of the most important skills that support discipline include the following:

- Quick-thinking before an action

- Carrying forward only one action at a time – One has to pick-up a ball before it is thrown

- Trusting one's good instincts

- Adapting under pressure

- Self-management and control

- Submitting to one's coach/manager – part of submission

- Following instructions - obedience

- Working with a team - collaboration

- Accepting correction

- Self evaluation and admitting to one's weaknesses

- Practice, practice, practice, for only in practicing is one's skills honed.

Read the following life story and share with a peer what three significant lessons you have learned from the story.

Orel Hershiser- A Man of Discipline

One of baseball's most disciplined players we have seen is the doughty Orel Hershiser. He has been one of baseball's most fierce competitors, and earned himself the nickname "Bulldog", from his team manager Tommy Lasorda. Hershiser's pitching talents were first noticed at Bowling Green State University in Bowling Green, Ohio. He was selected by the Los Angeles Dodgers in the 17th round of the 1979 amateur draft and assigned to their farm team in Clinton, Iowa. After four more seasons in the minor leagues with San Antonio and Albuquerque, Hershiser was called up to the Dodgers on September 1, 1983.

He had a breakthrough season in *1985* when he led the *National League* in winning percentage. His best season was *1988* when he led the league in *wins* (23), innings (267), and completed games (15). He finished that season with a record 59 consecutive scoreless innings pitched, breaking the record held by Dodger great *Don Drysdale*. In his final start of the year on *September 28*, he needed to pitch 10 shutout innings to set the mark—meaning not only that he would have to prevent the *San Diego Padres* from scoring, but that his own team would also need to fail to score in order to ensure *extra innings*. The Dodgers' anemic offense was obliging, however, and Hershiser pitched the first 10 innings of a scoreless tie, with the Padres eventually prevailing 2–1 in 16 innings. Hershiser almost did not pitch in the 10th inning, in deference to Drysdale, but was convinced by the Hall of Famer to take the mound and try to break the record. After averaging over 250 innings per season from 1985–89, the slender Hershiser broke down from overwork in *1990* when he tore *ligaments* in his elbow. He returned after the injury plagued year, still an excellent pitcher, but he never regained his level of brilliance of the late 1980s. In *1995* he joined the *Cleveland Indians*, and posted a 16–6 mark to play a pivotal role in helping the team reach the World Series for the first time since *1954*; he was also 14–6 for the *1997* pennant-winning Indians. He later joined the *San Francisco Giants* (*1998*) and *New York Mets* (*1999*) before rejoining the Dodgers for a final season in *2000*. In his career, Hershiser had a 204–150 regular season record with 2,014 *strikeout*s and an *ERA* of 3.48. In retirement, Hershiser served as a pitching coach for the Texas Rangers.

If one should interview Hershiser about his success he would probably say that his disciplined attitude accounted for his success. He had the discipline to stay away from drug usage and from other destructive behaviors that have destroyed the lives of some of his contemporaries. He might say too that his discipline was supported by his Christian faith to which he adhered throughout his career. Winning a ball game was important but, for him, faith was more important. As a guest star on an episode of the Christian children's video series *McGee and Me,* he starred in the part "Take Me Out to the Ball Game". After leaving the limelight of baseball he argued that sometimes it is easier to practice one's faith in the public than in private. However, he has not given up his faith. He shares in activities that still nurture his faith. (With some modifications, the biography of Oral Heirsheizer was taken from Wikipedia).

ACTIVITY I

Place an A if you agree and a D if you disagree with the following comments. Explain your responses to your friend.

1. _____"Discipline is the bridge between goals and accomplishment."- Jim Rohn

2. _____Discipline means that one learns how to order or manage one's life with the aim of finding one's destination.

3. _____Some aspects of discipline include: self-restraint, time management, and relationship building.

4. _____Management and overcoming distractions are important for development of discipline.

5. _____Maintaining a well balanced life requires the pain of discipline.

6. _____"No pain, no gain."

ACTIVTY II

Reflect on your attitude by putting "Yes" or "No" beside each question below.

1. Do you often take time to develop your skills, talents, gifts, potentials? _____

2. Does your time for development pass away without a sense of loss? _____

3. Do you make decisions to use your time according to your priorities? _____

4. Do you have an orderly way of managing your life? _____

5. Do you maintain a calendar or a "to do list?" _____

6. Do emergencies take away your focus on what is most important? _____

ACTIVTY III

Make a list of all the appointments that you have kept in the last two weeks and say how you feel about your:

1. Punctuality_____

2. Absence_____

3. Reliability_____

GOD'S MAP FOR THE DISCIPLINE OF YOUR LIFE

Joseph: A Man of Discipline

Joseph's life demonstrates much discipline. He could have had all the potential in the world, but he would not have achieved what he did, as governor of Egypt, without his personal-discipline. When Mrs. Potiphar tried to trap him with her sexual advances, he chose to run away. He did not seek to live by the laws of self-gratification. He understood that discipline was the path to his personal growth. It took a lot to resist a beautiful woman; a woman with money, and a woman with a lot of charm. But Joseph valued his life more than the immediate gratification. Not only did he show his discipline on that singular occasion, but also on the larger stages of his life he proved to be a man of discipline. When he was falsely accused and thrown into prison his disciplined life was made evident to his fellow prisoners. No wonder that when the butler and the baker had their dreams they went to him for their dreams' interpretation. Yes, people do watch us to see whether or not a person embraces positive attitudes. Successful people know that such attitudes are of the highest significance. Joseph knew that he could not just live as he wanted or pleased; he understood the power of discipline and dared to discipline himself.

When he became governor of Egypt and his brothers came to buy food, Joseph put them through a series of tests that sometimes seemed vengeful, but deeper reflection made it clear that what he was doing was to test their discipline. Had they grown? Were they still caught up in any vengeful actions? Had they stopped their sibling jealousies? Were they still ready to blame and deceive anyone they could? Were they ready to take responsibility for their past or present actions? Could they now be trusted? When Joseph received the answers to the forgoing questions he revealed himself to his brothers. It took him much discipline to constrain himself from divulging who he was through the time of the tests. However, he persisted in his restraint because he was truly disciplined- he had a goal in mind. As the famous American Football coach Oail Andrew (Bum) Phillips said, "The only discipline that lasts is self-discipline." Of course, when individuals cannot discipline themselves, and are not willing to be subjected to the discipline of those who are set in immediate authority over them, then they generally pay a big price when society calls them to discipline through punishment that often seems overbearing.

> *With Joseph in charge, he did not concern himself with anything except the food he ate.*

"If you desire that your conduct be good and kept from all evil, beware of all fits of bad temper. This is a sad malady which leads to discord, and there is no more life at all for the one who falls into it. For it brings quarrels between fathers and mothers, as between brothers and sisters; it makes the husband and wife abhor each other; it contains all wickedness; it encloses all injuries. When a man takes justice for his rule, walks in her ways, and dwells with her, there is no room left for bad temper." *-The Instruction of Ptah-Hotep, Precept XIX*

Note what the Bible quotes say about the disciplined life. Check the quote you like best.

1. Obedience to the Lord

   Proverbs 10:17- *"He who heeds discipline shows the way to life, but whoever ignores correction leads others astray."*

2. Following directions

   Proverbs 12:1-*"Whoever loves discipline loves knowledge, but he who hates correction is stupid."*

3. The Price of being obedient

   Proverbs 13:18- *"He who ignores discipline comes to poverty and shame, but whoever heeds correction is honored."*

4. Honor the words of your parents

   Proverbs 15:5-*"A fool spurns his father's discipline, but whoever heeds correction shows prudence."*

5. Accepting criticism

   Proverbs 15:32- *"He who ignores discipline despises himself, but whoever heeds correction gains understanding."*

6. The discipline of listening

   Proverbs 9:8- *"The wise in heart accept commands, but a chattering fool comes to ruin."*

7. The discipline of moral integrity

   Proverbs 10:9- *"The man of integrity walks securely, but he who takes crooked paths will be found out."*

8. The discipline of obedience

   Proverbs 30: 17- *"The eye that mocks a father, that scorns obedience to a mother, will be pecked out by the ravens of the valley, will be eaten by the vultures."* The discipline of learning

   Proverbs 1:5- *"Let the wise listen and add to their learning, and let the discerning get guidance."*

   Proverbs 9:9- *"Instruct a wise man and he will be wiser still; teach a righteous man and he will add to his learning."*

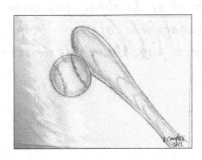

Look at the Diamond below and ask yourself about your personal discipline. Let the words around the mirror help you.

**HOW WELL DO
YOU MANAGE
YOUR TIME?**

**HOW EFFECTIVELY
DO YOU CONTROL
YOUR EMOTIONS?**

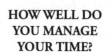

**HOW WELL DO
YOU APPLY YOUR
TRAINING?**

*Do you like what you have seen?
After you look back at the things you have seen concerning your focus and management of your discipline, respond to the questions on the next page that truly describe your discipline.*

TRANSFORMING YOUR ROAD MAP

1. Describe how you see yourself in terms of personal discipline?

2. What do you see might be the greatest obstacle affecting your practice of personal discipline?

3. What traits do you possess that you feel might help you best in developing a disciplined life?

4. What do you consider some weaknesses that hinder your efforts to be a well disciplined person?

5. If you need some help to be a disciplined person, what might that help be?

6. Who do you think might best help you to develop the habits of discipline that you might need?

"Too often we . . . enjoy the comfort of opinion without the discomfort of thought."

- John F. Kennedy

THE PRAYER OF A SPORTSMAN

By Benton Braley

Dear Lord, in the battle that goes on through life
I ask but a field that is fair,
A chance that is equal with all in the strife,
A courage to strive and to dare;

And if I should win, let it be by the code
With my faith and my honor held high;
And if I should lose, let me stand by the road,
And cheer as the winners go by.

And Lord, may my shouts be ungrudging and clear,
A tribute that comes from the heart,
And let me not cherish a snarl or a sneer
Or play any sniveling part;

Let me say, "There they ride, on whom laurel's bestowed
Since they played the game better than I."
Let me stand with a smile by the side of the road,
And cheer as the winners go by.

So grant me to conquer, if conquer I can,
By proving my worth in the fray,
But teach me to lose like a regular man,
And not like a craven, I pray;

Let me take off my hat to the warriors who strode
To victory splendid and high,
Yea, teach me to stand by the side of the road
And cheer as the winners go by.

Conclusion: This discussion is about discipline or a sense of control.

Discipline has a profound effect on people's character.

Discipline causes people to stay away from obsessions and addictions.

When one is disciplined, one can stay a course in face of failure.

Can you say, how disciplined you are?

DILIGENCE

"The heights by great men reached and kept, was not attained by sudden flight, but they while their companions slept were toiling through the night."

- Henry Wadsworth Longfellow

UNDERSTANDING YOUR EMOTIONAL STATE

When one is seeking to build an effective (winning) baseball team, all those who are involved in recruiting, managing, coaching, and playing must have one word on their minds - diligence. Before a recruiter recruits a prospect, he/she must be diligent in looking at the skills and attitude of the prospect. One must look at the ways in which the prospect develops by asking several questions: What is the probability that the prospect will get to the park on time? Does the prospect have good work (practice) ethics? Does the prospect pay attention to little things, try to learn good habits and correct bad habits? Is the prospect willing to listen to instructions? Is the prospect willing to change any bad habit? Does the prospect have a good team spirit? What is the attitude of the prospect on and off the field? Such is the kind of intense search that has to be carried out to ensure that when the prospect joins a team the team will be a winning one.

There is no celebration without Diligence

Each year, after a few games are played, it always becomes clear which teams have been selected with due diligence. When due diligence has not been achieved, panic often sets in and fans become frustrated. It is always of interest when one listens to the analysis, the evaluation and explanations that are usually given for the failures of a team, especially when diligence has not been practiced. Often, managers get fired, but if the truth be told, the team was poorly selected in the first place.

Of course, diligence is not being reflected on as a reality concerning the eyes of baseball scouts or managers, but the reflection needs to be focused directly on individual players. Every player has to ask himself, how diligent am I? How much effort am I making regarding my work? How well do I budget my time? How effectively do I monitor my activities? How well have I learned to concentrate? How well have I been practicing my game? An entire team might not be diligent in itself, however, when each individual is personally diligent such diligence impacts the whole team.

Read the following life story and share with a peer what three significant lessons you have learned from the story.

Mr. Diligence - Reggie Jackson

Reggie Jackson, (Reginald Martinez), nicknamed Mr. October, and one whom we have chosen to dub "Mr. Diligence," is a retired major league player, famously known for his clutch hitting. He played for 20 seasons with five different baseball teams (the New York Yankees, the Oakland A's, Baltimore Orioles, Kansas City Royals, and the California Angels). He helped win three consecutive World Series titles as a member of the Oakland A's in the early 1970s and also helped win two consecutive titles with the New York Yankees. He was inducted into the Baseball Hall of Fame in 1993.

Reggie's father, Martinez Jackson, who was a second baseman with the Newark Eagles of the Negro Leagues, instilled in his son much discipline. Martinez raised his son as a single parent after divorcing Reggie's mother. The young Jackson spent much time in practicing the game. He developed good habits. He tried to be the best at whatever he did. Anything else about him seems incomplete when compared to others. (With some modifications, the biography of Reggie Jackson was taken from Wikipedia).

> *"There are three types of baseball players: those who make it happen, those who watch it happen, and those who wonder what happens."*
> — *Tommy Lasorda*

ACTIVITY I

Read each question then give your response.

1. How long are you willing to work at a task before you give up?

2. Are you easily discouraged? _____ Yes _____ No _____ Sometimes _____

3. When life gets demanding do you feel to quit? _____ Yes _____ No _____ Sometimes

4. Do you believe in excellence? _____ Yes _____ No _____ Sometimes

5. Do you often settle for mediocrity? _____ Yes _____ No _____ Sometimes

6. Do you care enough about what you do? _____ Yes _____ No _____ Sometimes

7. Write a paragraph and share with a colleague what your answers say about yourself

ACTIVITY II

Look at the following sayings of the wise and describe what each mean to you.

1. "[Diligence is] the mother of good fortune and ideas, its opposite, never brought a man to the goal of any of his best wishes." – Miguel DeCervantes.

2. "When life knocks you down you have two choices – stay down or get up." - (Tom Krause).

3. "If you are willing to do only what is easy, life will be hard. But if you are willing to do what is hard, life will be easy." – T. Harve Eker

4. "Training and managing your own mind is the most important skill you could ever own." – T. Harve Eker

ACTIVTY III

1. Can you share an experience in which you had to exercise much diligence in order to achieve your goal?

2. Describe a time when you were insulted or humiliated by a thoughtless comment. How did you react?

3. Talk about a time when you saw someone being disrespected, and explain how you reacted.

GOD'S MAP FOR YOUR DILIGENCE

"The scribe who is skilled in his office, He is found worthy to be a courtier."

-The Instruction of Ptah-Hotep, 27:16–17

Joseph: A Man of Diligence

If for no other life, the above comments were true, and it is also true of Joseph's. His diligence brought him into the presence of Pharaoh and allowed him to become the second most powerful person in Egypt. His diligence was made manifest through his service in the house of Potiphar and even more manifest as he served as governor. There might be persons who have risen to high positions because of their political connections, but not so with Joseph. He came from the "pit" (prison) to the governorship. One cannot imagine him getting to his position and holding it by being lazy or apathetic. The evidence is that during the seven years of plenty and the seven years of famine he worked diligently and untiringly to make sure everything was in place so that the country would not starve. The life of the people of Egypt rested in Joseph's hand and he delivered. In Genesis 41:41-49 we read:

> *So the warden put Joseph in charge of all those held in the prison, and he was made responsible for all that was done there. The warden paid no attention to anything under Joseph's care, because the LORD was with Joseph and gave him success in whatever he did.*

So Pharaoh said to Joseph, "I hereby put you in charge of the whole land of Egypt.' Then Pharaoh took his signet ring from his finger and put it on Joseph's finger. He dressed him in robes of fine linen and put a gold chain around his neck. He had him ride in a chariot as his second-in-command, and men shouted before him, make way!" Thus he put him in charge of the whole land of Egypt.

Then Pharaoh said to Joseph, 'I am Pharaoh, but without your word no one will lift hand or foot in all Egypt.' Pharaoh gave Joseph the name Zaphenath-Paneah and gave him Asenath daughter of Potiphara, priest of On, to be his wife. And Joseph went throughout the land of Egypt.

Joseph was thirty years old when he entered the service of Pharaoh king of Egypt. He went out from Pharaoh's presence and traveled throughout Egypt. During the seven years of abundance the land produced plentifully. Joseph collected all the food produced in those seven years of abundance and stored it in the cities. He put the food grown in the fields in surrounding cities. He stored up huge quantities of grain, like the sand of the sea; it was so much that he stopped keeping records because it was beyond measure.

Some people become arrogant when they attain a high position, but not Joseph; he remained fervent and earnest regarding his work. No one could accuse him of not giving the 40 hours per week which we use as the model of our work week today. Joseph went about his work meticulously. He did not make excuses for his failures and then blame them on others. Joseph had great interest in whatever he did, thus bringing his dreams to fulfillment.

If one were to practice the admonitions as given in the biblical quotations that follow, one would be sure to become as diligent as Joseph. Read carefully and ponder each passage.

1. Learning diligence from nature

Proverbs 6:6- *"Go to the ant, thou sluggard; consider her ways, and be wise."*

2. One secret of the wealthy

Proverbs 10:4- *"Lazy hands make a man poor, but diligent hands bring wealth."*

Proverbs 21:5- *"The plans of the diligent leads to profit, as surely as haste leads to poverty."*

3. The result of idleness

Proverbs 12:24- *"Diligent hands will rule, but laziness ends in slave labor."*

4. Combination of physical and mental determination

Proverbs 13:4- *"The sluggard craves and gets nothing, but the desires of the diligent are fully satisfied."*

5. Success and diligence

Proverbs 22:29- *"Do you see a person diligent in his business? He shall stand before kings; he shall not stand before mean men."*

6. Diligence and emotions

Proverbs 4:23- *"Watch over your heart with all diligence, for from it flows the springs of life."*

On the Diamond of diligence, look at yourself to see what help you need.

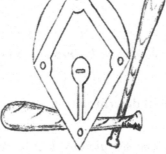

WORKING ON
SKILLS, LACKING TO
FOCUS ON THE TASK
AT HAND

NOT A QUITTER, BUT
WORKS HARD TO
REACH THE GOAL

WORKING
AGGRESSIVELY
TO OVERCOME
OBSTACLES ON
YOUR TRACK

Do you like what you have seen?
After you look back at the things you have seen concerning your
level of diligence, respond to the questions on the next page
giving honest answers.

TRANSFORMING YOUR ROAD MAP

1. Which of the following best describes your level of diligence?

   a.) Very diligent _____   **b.) Diligent** _____

   c.) Somewhat diligent _____   **d.) Not diligent** _____

   e.) Not sure _____

2. Where would you like to go from where you are?

3. If you answered a – e in question 1 tell what are the kinds of challenges that can impede your progress toward being a diligent person?

4. What areas of strengths do you believe you have that can build up your diligence?

5. What do you consider your greatest challenge on which you need to work in order to build up your level of diligence?

6. What kind of help do you need to correct the challenges you face in the area of diligence?

"The expectations of life depend upon diligence; the mechanic that would perfect his work must first sharpen his tools." - Confucius

WORDS TO PONDER

For three years your batting average has been .330, but in the last year your average has slipped to 205. It is being rumored that if you do not raise your average you will be sent to the Minors. Contemplate how the following would help you deal with the frustration.

"If you identify yourself with your failures, problems, and disappointments, you will probably become a failure."

– Denis Waitley.

Conclusion: This discussion is about diligence – that is, about one's capacity to overcome obstacles and frustrations.

Diligence means that capacity to work hard to finish a task.

A diligent person is not a slacker.

Can you say that you are a diligent person?

DEPENDABILITY

"*Dependability, integrity, the characteristic of never knowingly doing anything wrong, that you would never cheat anyone, that you would give everybody a fair deal. Character is a sort of an all-inclusive thing. If a man has character, everyone has confidence in him.*"

– Omar N. Bradley

CAN YOU TRUST YOURSELF?

Every serious baseball manager will tell you that when a game is on the line the pitcher that is called from the bullpen or the batter sent to the plate, is the one who has that great virtue of dependability. At the point when a game is on the line, it is not popular who is needed, but the one and determined. That player has attitude. Such a player is called have particular intuitiveness about shown, they have been this kind of *There is no celebration without being dependable* the player who is most flamboyant or who is most consistent, committed a dogged personality and mental "the clutch player." Baseball managers this kind of player, for as research has player themselves. When a manager faces a critical situation, and has to contemplate how much risk there is, he finds the most dependable player. While risks give place to new opportunities, dependability creates stability. A home run hitter might be great, but if such a hitter strikes out many times, the effective manager will choose the consistent doubles hitter who rarely strikes out.

Read the following life story and share with a peer what three significant lessons you have learned from the story.

Cal Ripkin Jr- Mr. Dependable

Cal Ripkin Jr. is a retired Major League Baseball shortstop and third baseman who played his entire career (1981–2001) for the Baltimore Orioles. During his baseball career, he earned the nickname "The Iron Man" for always remaining in the lineup despite numerous minor injuries, and for being reliable in showing up to work every day. He is perhaps best known for breaking New York Yankees first baseman, Lou Gehrig's record for consecutive games played - a record many deemed unbreakable. Ripken surpassed the 56-year-old record when he played in his 2,131st game on September 6, 1995. The game between the Orioles and California Angels was a sold-out crowd at Oriole Park, Camden Yards. To make the feat even more memorable,

Ripken hit a home run the previous night that tied Gehrig's record, and another home run in his 2,131st game, which fans later voted as Major League Baseball's "Most Memorable Moment." Ripken grew up in Aberdeen, Maryland, in a baseball family. His father, Cal Sr., was a long-time coach in baseball who managed the Orioles in the late 1980s. (With some modifications, the biography of Cal Ripkin was taken from Wikipedia).

> *"Early in my career, I decided I never wanted to get out of shape."*
> *– Cal Ripkin, Jr.*

ACTIVITY I- Shape your thoughts with a colleague about the following

1. How could Ripkin accomplish such feats?

2. Can anyone count on you in the same way that Ripkin could be counted on? Yes __ No___

3. Read the following story and share with your group what you think it says about dependability.

A certain young man was looking for a job. He went out into the country and was interviewed by a farmer. He had no references so when the farmer asked about his abilities his only response was "I can sleep on a stormy night." The farmer did not quite understand his response however, he gave him the job. The young man was shown the farm and all of the chores that he had to do. He was shown the barn in which the cattle were to be placed. He was shown the coups, for the poultry and the stable for the horses. The farmer hoped that all would be well.

One night, a heavy thunderstorm began and the farmer became worried. He wondered if his cattle, horses and other farm animals were safe. He got up and went to find the young man sound asleep in his room. The farmer tried to awaken him, but left in disgust, went back to his room, put on his farm clothes, took a lantern and went to the farm. As he carried out his search, he found that all was safe; the cows were in their barn, the horses in their stable and the chickens in their coups. On seeing that all was well, the farmer went back to bed. The next morning the farmer spoke to the boy, and asked whether or not he had heard the storm last night. The boy responded, "No, as I told you, I can sleep on a stormy night."

1. Whenever you get a job to do, do you ever finish it in a way that you feel satisfied?

    Yes _____ No _____

2. Are you someone who can be left without supervision? Yes _____ No _____ Why or why not? Explain.

    _____

    _____

3. Is your behavior consistent with your character traits that you have developed over the years? Explain.

    _____

4. What qualities do you possess that would make people feel safe around you?

    _____

    _____

5. When given a task, do you ever take it to completion in a way that makes you happy?

    _____

6. Write a short essay on a task that you enjoy and tell how you generally bring it to completion.

    _____

    _____

    _____

    _____

GOD'S MAP FOR A LIFE OF DEPENDABILITY

Joseph: A Man of Dependability

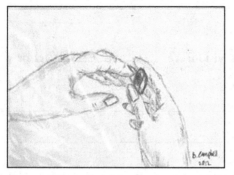

How does a king take a thirty year old young man and make him governor of Egypt? How does he put him in charge of a program to save the whole Egyptian nation from starvation? How does he tell him that he would be second in command? The biblical record says:

"So Pharaoh said to Joseph, 'I hereby put you in charge of the whole land of Egypt. Then Pharaoh took his signet ring from his finger and put it on Joseph's finger. He dressed him in robes of fine linen and put a gold chain around his neck. He had him ride in a chariot as his second-in-command, and men shouted before him, 'Make way!' Thus he put him in charge of the whole land of Egypt.

Then Pharaoh said to Joseph, 'I am Pharaoh, but without your word no one will lift hand or foot in all Egypt.' Pharaoh gave Joseph the name Zaphenath-Paneah and gave him Asenath daughter of Potiphara, priest of On, to be his wife. And Joseph went throughout the land of Egypt.

Joseph was thirty years old when he entered the service of Pharaoh king of Egypt . . ."
– Genesis 40:41-46.

The verses above are among the most powerful words that describe Joseph's character of DEPENDABILITY. Joseph proved that he could be trusted when he was left in charge of Potiphar's household. He proved his reliability while he was in jail and carried out his chores. He proved it when he became the governor of Egypt. Such a quality of dependability was likely showing when he was a lad at home.

> *But he refused. "With me in charge," he told her, "my master does not concern himself with anything in the house; everything he owns he has entrusted to my care.*

His father affirmed his trust when he sent the young Joseph far away from home to find his brothers. The quality of dependability might have been, in part, responsible for his brothers' jealousy. They might have derided him for such dependability. We see it all the time, how the quality of dependability allows people of integrity to pay attention to those so blessed, while leading the irresponsible to jealousy. One of the struggles in some communities today, among certain classes, is that of making mockery of those who make high achievements in school. The mockers say if you make good grades you are "kissing up" to the system. As a matter of fact, they are dubbed as "nerds," "queer" or other such names.

It should be noted that the gift of dependability is not something given to one at birth. It is something that one must seek to develop. The dependable person is not just reliable when persons in authority are around. It is not a quality that is shown when one is under supervision, but it shines in the dark, when a supervisor is not around. The dependable person gets things done without constant nagging and pushing.

Pay close attention to the scriptural verses below noting their encouragement to be dependable.

1. Honest work leads to greater rewards

Proverbs 11:18- *"The wicked man earns deceptive wages, but he who sows righteousness reaps a sure reward."*

2. Beauty in the eyes of the Lord

Proverbs 14:8- *"Charm is deceptive, and beauty is fleeting; but a woman who fears the Lord is to be praised."*

Proverbs 12:20- *"There is **deceit** in the hearts of those who plot evil, but joy for those who promote peace."*

3. The spirit of Loyalty

Proverbs 25:13- *"As the cold of snow in the time of harvest so is a faithful messenger to them that send him: for he refreshes the soul of his masters."* (KJV)

4. The danger of depending on the undependable

Proverbs 25:19- *"Confidence in an unfaithful man in time of trouble is like a broken tooth, and a foot out of joint."*

5. Mercy and truth

Proverbs 20:28- ***"Love** and **faithfulness** keep a king safe; through love his throne is made secure."*

6. Cheaters never prosper

Proverbs 17:20- *"A man of perverse heart does not prosper; he whose tongue is **deceitful** falls into trouble."*

On the Diamond of Dependability, look at yourself to see what help you need.

**DO YOU HONOR
YOUR WORDS WITH
WHAT YOU
DO?**

**ARE YOU
CONSCIENTIOUS IN
WHAT YOU
DO?**

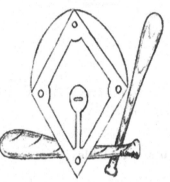

**ARE YOU TRUE TO
THE TASK OR THE
GOAL YOU HAVE
SET?**

*Do you like what you have seen?
After you look back at the things you have seen concerning
your dependability, respond to the questions on the next
page concerning such a trait.*

TRANSFORMING YOUR ROAD MAP

1. Circle the one that best describes the kind of person you think you are

    a. Very dependable

    b. Somewhat dependable

    c. Not dependable

    d. Not sure

2. Where do you think your attitude of dependability will take you?

3. Are there situations in your life that make it difficult for you to be dependable?

    a. Name any of those situations.

    b. How can you change those situations?

    c. Or if the situations cannot change, what else might you do?

4. Name three areas that relate to dependability?

    a. _____

    b. _____

    c. _____

5. If you have challenges in being a dependable person, what help do you need to transform your situation?

"Once you say you're going to settle for second, that's what happens to you in life, I find."
                                                        - John F. Kennedy

You have been given several videos to watch in order to analyze pitchers with whom you have trouble. However, you feel you already know what the problems are. You feel that the videos are quite boring and that you would be better off texting your friends or watching other videos that are much more exciting. No one is watching you but you feel you have to overcome the struggles of your divided mind, and demonstrate your dependability. Think of how the following thought might transform your attitude. "He who does nothing renders himself incapable of doing anything, but while we are executing any work we are preparing and qualifying ourselves to undertake another." – William Hazlitt

Conclusion: This discussion is about dependability – that is the virtue of consistency

The point we made again and again is that some people can do a task for a short time, but they do not have the capacity to do their job year after year.

We are interested in the process you use to achieve and maintain goals.

We also want to know concerning your level of loyalty.

DEVELOPMENT

"Be not afraid of growing SLOWLY; be afraid only of standing still."

- Chinese Proverb

ARE YOU ALWAYS WILLING TO LEARN?

One of the things that is constantly evaluated in baseball players and managers or players and managers in other games, is how well they develop over time. It is quite obvious when a player develops from one year to another. Where was the player in his/her first year? What has he/she accomplished by their second, third, fourth, fifth and following years? When do they begin to fall off? What strategies do they apply to sustain them in times when things are difficult? These are crucial questions asked in order to determine how well a player has developed his/her skills. If a player does not demonstrate development or growth, he will be off the team in a short time - that is either traded or cut from the team. It is interesting to note that it is not only capability that determines one's ability so much, as development. Many players are capable, they have great intelligence but they do not spend time to develop. Development focuses on how hard one is willing to work to hone one's skills. IQ is one thing, but that is a very small aspect of intelligence.

There is no celebration without self-development

As part of the process for excellence, one constantly needs to assess and evaluate what skill levels one needs to develop. For example:

- What tools might I require to enhance my personal development?

- What kind of mentorship do I need?

- What level of mental maturity do I need for the task?

- Is my emotional maturity suited for the task? How stable or balanced are my emotions?

- How developed are my social maturity?

- How respectful and responsible in my sexual interactions?

- How effective am I with money management? _____

- How mature am I in my faith relationships? _____

- Am I a responsible moral agent? _____

Read the following life story and share with a peer what three significant lessons you have learned from the story.

George Herman Ruth, Jr. - A Symbol of Self-Development

"Babe Ruth" - George Herman Ruth Jr., is known as one of America's most famous baseball players. He was born on February 6, 1895 in Baltimore, Maryland. He was one of eight children born to George Herman Ruth and Kate Schamberger. Of the eight, only George Jr. and a sister, Mamie, survived. Ruth's father owned a tavern, and running the business left him and his wife with little time to watch over their children. Young George began skipping school and getting into trouble. He also played baseball with other neighborhood children whenever possible.

At the age of seven, Ruth was sent to the St. Mary's Industrial School for Boys - a school that took care of boys who had problems at home. It was run by the Brothers (men who had taken vows to lead religious lives) of a Catholic Order of teachers. Ruth wound up staying there on and off until he was almost twenty. At St. Mary's, Ruth studied, worked in a tailor shop, and learned values such as sharing and looking out for smaller, weaker boys. He also developed his baseball skills with the help of one of the Brothers.

Ruth became so good at baseball (both hitting and as a left-handed pitcher) that the Brothers wrote a letter to Jack Dunn, manager of the Baltimore Orioles Minor League Baseball Team, inviting him to come see Ruth. After watching Ruth play for half an hour, Dunn offered him a six-month contract for six hundred dollars. Dunn also had to sign papers making him Ruth's guardian until the boy turned twenty-one.

When Dunn brought Ruth to the Oriole's locker room for the first time in 1914, one of the team's coaches said, "Well, here's Jack's newest babe now!" The nickname stuck, and Babe Ruth stuck with the team as well. Ruth performed so well that he was moved up later that year to the Boston Red Sox of the American League. Ruth pitched on championship teams in 1915 and 1916, but he was such a good hitter that he was switched to the outfield so that he could play every day. (Pitchers usually play only every four or five days because of the strain that pitching has on their throwing arm.) In 1919, his twenty-nine home runs set a new record and led to the beginning of a new playing style. Up to that point, home runs occurred very rarely, and baseball's best players were usually pitchers and high-average "singles" hitters.

By 1920 Ruth's frequent home runs made the "big bang" style of play more popular and successful. He broke into the major leagues with the Boston Red Sox as a starting pitcher, but after he was sold to the New York Yankees in 1919, he converted to a full-time right fielder and subsequently became one of the league's most prolific hitters. He was a mainstay in the Yankees' lineup that won seven pennants and four World Series titles during his tenure with the team. After a short stint with the Boston Braves in 1935, he retired. In 1936, he was voted as one of the first five players into to the Baseball Hall of Fame.

What is most notable about Ruth is not how many home runs he hit or how well he could pitch, but that he faced many obstacles and overcame them and developed to become one of America's greatest baseball players. (With some modifications, the biography of George Herman Ruth taken from Wikipedia).

> *"To succeed you must first improve, to improve you must first practice, to practice you must first learn, and to learn you must first fail." – Wesley Woo*

ACTIVITY I

1. Do you have an understanding as to how you are developing in any stage of your own life?

   Yes _____ No _____ No sure _____ Do not care _____

2. Do you have the kind of attitude that can take you through life's stages of development? _____

3. What are your goals for the development of your life? _____

   _____

   _____

4. How do you see yourself growing each day? _____

   _____

5. What are you doing today that might help with your development in a positive way? _____

   _____

6. What are you doing that might impact your development in a negative way? _____

   _____

7. What new skills have you learned in the last year that have aided your development? _____

   _____

8. Do you know another language other than your mother tongue? _____

   _____

9. When last have you read a whole book through and through?_____

10. Do you ever set aside a day for reading a book or looking at an educational DVD? _____

ACTIVITY II

Read the following poem, and then tell how it connects to your understanding of development or maturity.

I HAVE GIVEN UP ON LEARNING

I've given up [on] learning and ended my worries.
Given up my "yes" and given up my "no."
How great is the distance between right and wrong?
What nonsense to fear what others fear!
Yet others are all so very happy,
Feasting on the sacrificed ox in the fall,
Climbing up to the tower in the spring,
While I alone drift mutely along
Like a babe who has not learned to smile,
Like a waif without a home.
Others have more than they need,
While I alone have nothing.
What a fool am I! How confused am I!
Others are so very strong,
While I alone am weak.
Others are so very bright,
While I alone am dim.
So I drift along like the waves of the sea,
Like a restless, aimless wind.
Yes, others are teeming with plans and high causes
While I alone drift stubbornly on
Alone in my infantile Way,
Lapping up the milk of the Great Mother.
Annonymous

_____

_____

Read carefully the following quotes, then tell whether or not you agree (A) or disagree (D)

1. "Rich people constantly learn and grow. Poor people think they already know." T. Harve Eker
   _____

2. "If you think education is expensive, try ignorance." – A common motivational saying.
   _____

3. "Nothing in all the world is more dangerous than sincere ignorance and conscientious stupidity." Martin Luther King. Jr. _____

4. Name any steps that you have taken so that you might be a "Learn it all," rather than a "Know it all." (Extracted from a thought by T. Harve Eker). _____

B. Make a list of areas that you think you need to give more attention to for personal development.

1. _____

2. _____

3. _____

4. _____

5. _____

6. _____

7. _____

8. _____

9. _____

10. _____

GOD'S MAP FOR YOUR LIFE'S DEVELOPMENT

Joseph: A Man Who Diligently Developed Himself

Earlier, we made the point that such a positive gift as evident dependability in Joseph was not just a gift that came by chance, but like all his other gifts, came by diligent development. A common point made by commentators about Joseph is that before he was sold into Egyptian slavery, he was "a spoilt brat." While he lived at home his brothers saw him as a complainer and a "tattle tale." In fact, it can be established that his brothers' jealousy did not only have to do with the power of his dreams. It was not just that they felt that they were being told that one day they would have to bow down to him. It was not only that their father had given him the colorful princely coat.

> *"Now Joseph was well-built and handsome, after a while his master's wife took notice of Joseph and said, "'Come to bed with me!'"*

While the latter were extremely irritating, no one should discount his self-indulgent behavior. In fact, whatever else his father did helped to make him more indulgent. Through the harsh experience of being away from home among strangers, with people of a different culture and religious experience, Joseph was **forced to evaluate his life and adapt to the changes** necessary for survival and success.

We don't see this often, but not long ago a newspaper article spoke of a man who went to a police station and thanked them for arresting him some years earlier. Having gone to jail, he was able to turn his life around. At the time of writing he was one of the directors of services at the same prison where he had been locked up, and most exciting was that he was finishing his Ph.D.

Similarily, with Joseph it seems to take imprisonment for him to come to terms with his need for growth. He had to overcome his conceit. He had to learn that arrogance would not get him to go forward in life. Upon reaching Egypt, he had to learn new rules of life. He had to learn the courtesies that were necessary to serve in the house of the chief of Pharaoh's army. He had to learn the total way of life in Egypt. He had to learn the language. He had to learn the science and whatever else constituted the curriculum of Egyptian education. He had to learn how to preserve his integrity amidst the temptations of wealth in Potiphar's house. He had to learn what it meant to stay away from the debasing practices of Egypt. He had to learn to distrust himself and acknowledge his deficiencies in order that he would grow into mature manhood. He had to learn, and did learn. Yes, Joseph understood that growth or development meant learning; whether it is intellectual, social, relational, emotional, physical, moral, attitudinal, or spiritual, all development demand learning.

REFLECT ON THE IDEAS EMBEDDED IN THE FOLLOWING BIBLE QUOTES AND NOTE WHAT THEY SAY ABOUT YOUR PERSONAL DEVELOPMENT

1. **Wise people will always learn**

   Proverbs 9:9- *"Instruct a wise man and he will be wiser still; teach a righteous man and he will add to his learning."*

   Proverbs 1:5- "A wise man will hear, and will increase learning; and a man of understanding shall attain unto wise counsels."

   Proverbs 8:33- *"Hear instruction, and be wise, and refuse it not."*

   Proverbs 18:15- *"The heart of the discerning acquires knowledge; the ears of the wise seek it out."*

2. **Wise people will always stay in a circle of colleagues that can teach them something positive.**

   Proverbs 13:20- *"He who walks with the wise grows wise, but a companion of fools suffers harm."*

   Proverbs 17:17- *"A friend loves at all times, and a brother is born for adversity."*

   Proverbs 18:24- *"A man of many companions may come to ruin, but there is a friend who sticks closer than a brother. "*

   Proverbs 27:17- *"As iron sharpens iron, so one man sharpens another. "*

On the Diamond of Development look at yourself to see what help you need.

WHAT DOES YOUR GROWTH PLAN LOOK LIKE?

DO YOU MONITOR YOUR PERSONAL IMPROVEMENT?

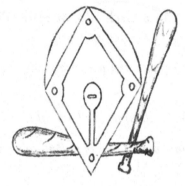

WHAT EFFECTIVE CHANGES DID YOU MAKE OVER THE LAST YEAR?

Do you like what you have seen?
After you look back at the things you have seen concerning your development, respond to the questions on the next page that truly describe your personal development.

GOD'S MAP FOR YOUR LIFE'S DEVELOPMENT

1. Circle the words that best describe your sense of satisfaction with your personal pattern of development.

    a. Very satisfied

    b. Satisfied

    c. A little satisfied

    d. Not satisfied

2. How much more growth or development would you like to see from where you are?

    _____

    _____

3. Name three obstacles affecting your ability to grow or develop in any aspect of your life.

    _____

    _____

4. What areas of strengths do you have that can heighten the possibility for your development?

    _____

    _____

5. If you answered question 3, tell the kind of help you might need to correct the challenges you face regarding your development.

    _____

    _____

"If you are not continuously learning you will be left behind" T. Harve Eker

WORDS TO PONDER

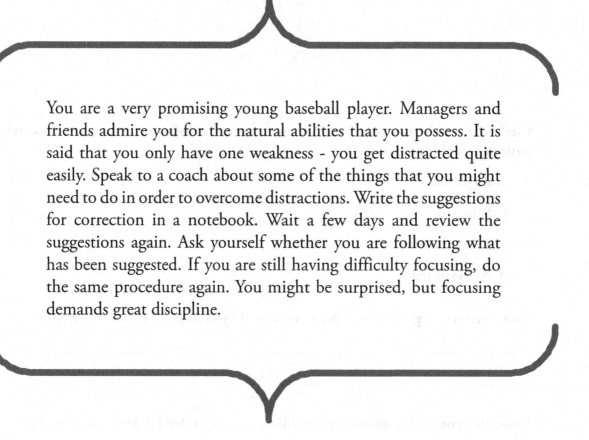

You are a very promising young baseball player. Managers and friends admire you for the natural abilities that you possess. It is said that you only have one weakness - you get distracted quite easily. Speak to a coach about some of the things that you might need to do in order to overcome distractions. Write the suggestions for correction in a notebook. Wait a few days and review the suggestions again. Ask yourself whether you are following what has been suggested. If you are still having difficulty focusing, do the same procedure again. You might be surprised, but focusing demands great discipline.

Conclusion: The point of this discussion is to focus on your personal development – that is, your willingness to move from small steps to larger steps in your growth. Have you taken any growth steps?

We are concerned about the development of your mind, body and soul - all in balance.

We want to know whether you would consider yourself one who seeks knowledge everyday, in every area of your life.

Take a look at your present skills and see whether they are better than what they were a year ago?

Do you engage in personal development on a constant basis?

It is said if you will not change, the world will change around you.

"The fundamental qualities for good execution of a plan is first, intelligence; then discernment and judgment, which enable one to recognize the best method as to attain it; the singleness of purpose, and, lastly, what is most essential of all, will stubborn will."

- Marshal Fernidand Foch

LEARNING TO SEE THE WORLD FOR WHAT IT IS

One of the things sports' commentators often talk about is managers' or players' instincts for their game. Baseball managers, players or persons of comparable games need profound instinct. Instinct means being wise, astute, sensible, intelligent, judicious, careful, thoughtful, sharp, intuitive, perceptive and discerning.

Discernment is most often used in the Christian culture where it connects to spiritual insight. It is recognized as a special gift of God that helps a person to identify truth from error, the holy from the unholy, good from evil, and the spirit of holiness from unclean spirits.

However, discernment has the more general conceptions as named above. We have heard our mothers say, they can see through a nine foot wall. That means they are profoundly intuitive. They can see beyond ordinary people. They are not easily fooled by deceptive individuals. While *There is no celebration without Discernment.* such intuition or discernment might be considered a gift, it still depends upon thoughtful observation, careful analysis, expert advice, and proficient study, etc. Discernment means more than being "street smart." It demands sound knowledge and understanding. This is why in baseball or other games so much effort is made to keep statistics. The more the statistics are reflected in the decisions, the greater the possibility that one will succeed. Of course, smart individuals who rely purely on technical data are sometimes wrong. So, this is where experience comes in. "Experience," it is said, "teaches wisdom." Hopefully we can all learn from our experience(s). However, our opinion is that there is more to wisdom than our experience(s), but for now we use experience as one of the great teachers in the game of life.

Read the following life story and share with a peer what three significant lessons you have learned from the story.

Jimmy Rollins - Discerning Jim

In looking at baseball players, it is hard to identify anyone of whom it can be said they have the highest level of wisdom and discernment. However, we dare present James Calvin "Jimmy" Rollins (born November 27, 1978 in Oakland, California), nicknamed "J-Roll", as a young man of great wisdom and discernment. Such wisdom and discernment are usually spoken of in baseball or other game language as very great "instinct" for the game. This is to say that Rollins has a tremendous inclination for the game and is believed to be able to play the game with profound sensitivity.

Rollins comes from an athletic family. He grew up watching his mother play competitive fast pitch softball for a Baptist Church group for many years. He credits the experience for helping him develop a cerebral approach to the game. He has been described as having "a near-photographic memory of games, at-bats and pitches. Though Rollins has developed into being an all-round player, his power hitting, and base running skill set him apart from many other players. He has stolen at least 20 bases every season since 2001, with a career high of 47 in 2008. Rollins, it is said, imitates his childhood baseball hero, Rickey Henderson.

In an article extolling the virtues of Rollins, baseball writer Alan Schwartz says:

> "*Anyone wondering where he got his charisma, confidence and mouth, need look no further than Gigi Rollins of Alameda, Calif., middle infielder for the Allen Temple Baptist Church women's fast-pitch softball team, now retired. She dazzled with the gloves and burned around the bases. It was at her spiked feet that young Jimmy learned both the game and the verve with which he plays it; baseball might cherish the image of fathers playing catch with sons, but Rollins owes everything to his mother.*" (With some modifications, the biography of Jimmy Rollins was taken from Wikipedia).

"You can't hit what you can't see."

-Walter Johnson

---

1. Look at the picture carefully then tell how each of the following words below help to shape your understanding of the picture.

a.) Discernment _____

_____

b.) Observation _____

_____

c.) Questioning _____

_____

d.) Investigation _____

_____

e.) Focused Attention _____

_____

2. Comment on what you think of the following sayings of the wise:

a.) "Discernment is about learning to separate truth from lies, illusion from reality, and fantasy from facts. It is about learning the difference between: emotional truth and Spiritual Truth; emotional impulse and intuitive guidance; being victimized and feeling like a victim. It is about recognizing the difference between a person that can be trusted and one who will betray us - between a soul connection and an emotional attraction to a person who is emotionally unavailable."– Robert Burney

b.) "A rich man may be wise in his own eyes, but a poor man who has discernment sees through him." - Anonymous.

c.) "The supreme purpose of education is expert discernment in all things, the power to tell the good from the bad, the genuine from the counterfeit, and to prefer the good and the genuine from the bad and counterfeit." - Education Quote

d.) "The fundamental qualities for good execution of a plan is first; intelligence; then discernment and judgment, which enable one to recognize the best method as to attain it; the singleness of purpose; and, lastly, what is most essential of all, will-stubborn will."- Marshal Ferdinand Foch

e.) Wisdom is your perspective on life, your sense of balance, your understanding of how the various parts and principles apply and relate to each other. It embraces judgment, discernment, and comprehension. It is a gestalt or oneness, and integrated wholeness." – Steven Covey

_____

_____

ACTIVTY II

1. Do you consider yourself a person of discernment?

    Yes _____ No _____ Not sure _____

2. Explain your response to # 1 _____

3. Can you distinguish between information, knowledge and wisdom? Yes _____ No _____

    Not sure _____

4. Do you know the difference between truth, a lie and a half truth? Yes _____ No _____

    Not sure _____ Explain

5. Do you recognize biases when you see them? Yes _____ No _____ Not sure _____

    Explain _____

6. Do you often get deceived - outsmarted? Yes _____ No _____ Never _____ Sometimes _____

7. If you were with a group of friends, would you be able to know when to pull away from the group?
    Yes _____ No _____ Not sure _____ Most difficult _____

8. If you answered "yes," list 3 things you looked for to make your decision.

   a. _____

   b. _____

   c. _____

9. Explain how an understanding of discernment can help you to make a distinction between the following:

   a. Truth and falsehood?

   b. Right and wrong?

   c. Genuine and ingenuous stuff?

   d. Authentic and inauthentic things?

10. From the following list, check the five insightful characteristics you would consider most essential for your day to day decisions?

   a. Thinking?

   b. Feeling?

   c. Setting boundary conditions?

   d. Weighting and measuring?

   e. Response feedback?

   f. Action orientation?

   g. Flexibility?

11. Discuss with your peer why you have chosen the one you have.

12. Name a few things against which you think it necessary to discriminate.

   a.

   b.

   c.

   d.

GOD'S MAP FOR YOUR LIFE'S DISCERNMENT

Joseph: A Man of Discernment

When one thinks of the gift of discernment, a catalogue of persons might come to mind. At the top of the list one would have to name Joseph. When he was placed in jail, the chief jailer recognized that there was something distinct about him. The Bible puts it this way, "The LORD was with him; he showed him kindness and granted him favor in the eyes of the prison warden." (See Genesis 39:21 NIV). Later the chief butler and the chief baker would recognize the same as he interpreted their dreams (Genesis 40). Sometime later, Pharaoh would come to recognize the same. When Pharaoh had his dream concerning the "seven fat cows and the seven thin cows;" the "seven fat ears and the seven thin ears," it was also Joseph who interpreted his dream. When Pharaoh called upon him to interpret his dream, Joseph noted that the wisdom was not in him, but from God. (Genesis 41:16). Pharaoh was so impressed by the evident correctness of his interpretation that he appointed him to be the second in command over the kingdom in order to carry out the plans that would bring about the fulfillment of his dream. Throughout his

> *"We both had dreams," they answered, "but there is no one to interpret them." Then Joseph said to them, "Do not interpretations belong to God? Tell me your dreams."*

governorship Joseph showed the depth of his wisdom as he staved off the seven years of the starvation which would have ravished the land. His wisdom was also evident in the way he dealt with his brothers as they went down to buy food in Egypt.

The point is clear that Joseph knew how to distinguish between the good and the bad. He was able to make appropriate moral choices. He understood the seductive nature of a corrupted culture. He recognized that self-trust created a path to failure. He understood that the wisest of counseling comes from God.

It is one thing to have a great amount of knowledge, but knowledge without wisdom will turn a person into a big fool. Likely, you might know a lot of people with many degrees, but they have little "common sense," or what is called, "street smart." Likely, you have also seen individuals who are called "great intellectuals" but turn their backs on the source of wisdom. The Bible clearly states, "The fear of the Lord, that is wisdom" (Proverbs 9:10). Such a "fear" or respect was well-known to Joseph. Father Jacob had set the example by introducing him to the true God and he carried his belief into Egypt.

Of interest, is the fact that some four hundred years afterward, a later Pharaoh who had not known Joseph (Exodus 1:8; Acts 7:8), made the lives of the Israelites so miserable that God sent Moses and Aaron to call for their release. The Egyptian Wisemen sought to compete with Moses who claimed the wisdom of God, but they failed in the many feats that would constitute the ten plagues that the Egyptian wise men had to call it quits because they could not compete. They had to admit that the God of Israel was more powerful than they were.

Read the following passages carefully and note their connection to discernment. Search the book of Proverbs to find other such passages if you will.

The fear of God as the source of wisdom

Proverbs 9:10- *"The fear of the Lord is the beginning of wisdom, and knowledge of the Holy One is understanding."*

Wisdom and discernment

Proverbs 10:13- *"Wisdom is found on the lips of the discerning, but a rod is for the back of him who lacks judgment."*

Proverbs 14:33- *"Wisdom reposes in the heart of the discerning and even among fools she lets herself be known."*

Proverbs 16:21- *"The wise in heart are called discerning, and pleasant words promote instruction."*

Wisdom and the heart of a fool

Proverbs 15:14- *"The discerning heart seeks knowledge, but the mouth of a fool feeds on folly."*

Proverbs 14:6 - *"The mocker seeks wisdom and finds none, but knowledge comes easily to the discerning."*

Proverbs 29:11- *"A fool gives full vent to his anger, but a wise man keeps himself under control."*

Proverbs 18:13- *"He who answers before listening- that is his folly and his shame."*

After reading the passages above, tell what kind of person you are or wish to be.

_____

_____

_____

On the Diamond of Discernment look at yourself and see what help you need.

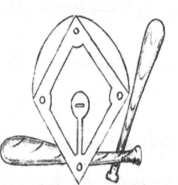

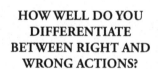

HOW CRITICAL ARE YOUR INSIGHTS IN THE TASKS IN WHICH YOU ENGAGE?

HOW MUCH AWARENESS DO YOU HAVE OF YOUR ENVIRONMENT?

HOW WELL DO YOU DIFFERENTIATE BETWEEN RIGHT AND WRONG ACTIONS?

Do you like what you have seen?
After you look back at the things you have seen concerning your discernment, respond to the questions on the next page that truly describe your insightfulness or power of discerning.

TRANSFORMING YOUR ROAD MAP

1. Do you consider yourself a person with strong discerning skills? Explain your answer.

2. In what ways do you think the skill of discernment has been, or will be helpful to you in achieving your life's goals?

3. What do you see that might become the greatest obstacle affecting your capacity for discernment?

4. What skills do you have or would like to have that can enhance your level of discernment?

5. What kind of help would you like to have to correct any challenges that you might be facing in regards to discernment?

"When the well's dry, we know the worth of water." - **Benjamin Franklin**

Conclusion: The point of this discussion is about discernment – that is about people with genuinely deep insight.

Discernment often teaches a person how to act, how to deal with adversity, and how to manage conflict.

Do you see any need for the development of discernment in your map of life?

It takes a discerning eye to be effective
at hitting a ball.

DIGNITY

"Remember this, - that there is a proper dignity and proportion to be observed in the performance of every act of life."

- Marcus Aurelius

HAVE YOU SEEN YOURSELF FOR WHO YOU ARE?

Have you taken notice of the uniforms worn by baseball players? You might not know anything about the history of the uniforms; however, 4000 uniform styles have been tried since 1876. The outcome is that players today are expected to dress in uniforms that are carefully styled, properly measured. In addition, uniforms should present good taste, be modest, be conservative, and very distinct. One might ask, "Why such emphasis is given to uniforms? The simple answer is that uniforms give people or teams, identity, character and personality. Uniforms give a good appearance, and project very profound images. Advertisers and marketers like to say, "Image is everything." That might be an exaggeration and one might wish to debate it, but cannot contest for long that **image counts.**

What's behind the clothing?

Of course, while uniforms and other types of clothing count for a lot, one needs to ask, "What's behind the clothing?" Clothing says a lot about image. **Dignity** has to do with **image.** It has to do with how one is perceived in other's eyes; how one is esteemed and honored, how one is valued and respected, how one is admired and accepted in the public's eye. In the short term, such esteem and honor might be created by one's clothing. But we have a greater interest than talking about clothing or uniform. We are not only seeking to focus on clothing but on what is inside. A dignified person will not only be conscious of his/her outward appearance, but also about what is inside, about character and integrity.

> *There is no celebration without dignity and integrity*

Drugs and addictions

Integrity has to do with honesty. Thus, when one reads the story of baseball, especially about the years of steroids in Senator Mitchell's report, one feels a profound sense of frustration, for what had been the most respected pass time in American life. The fact is that the competitive nature of the game, the desire for fame, success, strength, power, speed, self-confidence, overcome insecurities and fear and obtain a larger and larger contract, have allowed many players that could have been held in high respect to take steroids and growth hormones. What was gained in the short term, have left many with tarnished lives, broken families, some developing high blood pressure, high cholesterol, heart attacks, cancers and other life threatening conditions. In effect, the consequences for the wrong drugs have been grave.

Violence

When we do surveys of games that youngsters like to play these days, we find an enormous interest in the more violent games. When we ask why, we are told that it is fun. It is an interesting fact too that many of the games such as baseball, football, hockey, basketball that are played for public entertainment have become so associated with violence. Yes, it is true that we seem to be living today in "a culture of violence." However, dignified people learn that violence is a destruction of any effective goal achievement. This of what is happening in what is called the gladiator's game, football and make not that even though many players have achieved what they would can their goal, that the injuries they suffer and their short life make the achievement hollow. The same can be said of the war games that are played on the internet. It can be very frustrating when the game is over the question is usually raised as to what really was achieved. Most of the time the answer is clear that "violence only begets violence." Not much else is achieved. Whether in the games we play or in the game of life, we have to learn to **stop the violence** before it destroys all of us.

Sexual discretion

It is said that because baseball players, apart from being the pin-up boys of one of the most popular and exciting games, are paid handsomely, lead the life of celebrities and generally look handsome, they become one of the most desired partners for dating. If they are not discretionate, their reputations and careers can be destroyed by those who are seeking to relate to them just for a "hit." By "hit" we mean indiscriminate sexual relation. It is of interest that advice is given to young girls on how to stake out the players in baseball games so that relationships can develop. The girls are told to visit the home games since players have to be there for 81 games a year, not to mention near-daily training, workouts, practices and meetings. They are taught to check out team websites so they can know what time the stadium gates open, both on game days and off-days and then get their early. Such effort will give them time to meet a pro they have been eying- most likely after batting practice. All of these strategies are tried to develop a relationship. And if the possibility opens itself they will offer themselves sexually. How many players resist the offer? Few, we have been told. And what is the cost of a wrong decision to their career? We know too many players who have been tarnished through sexual indiscretion and instead of playing the game they spend a lot of time trying to clear their names.

Read the following life story and share with a peer what three significant lessons you have learned from the story.

Jackie Robinson - Man of High Dignity and Integrity

We do not know that Jack Robinson was never caught in any of the above indiscretions, but we have chosen him as a model of dignity and integrity. He was born in Cairo, Georgia in 1919 to a family of sharecroppers. His father left home not long after he was born and his mother, Mallie Robinson, single-handedly raised him and four siblings. They were the only black family on their block, and the prejudice they encountered only strengthened their bond. Of course, the racial discrimination became so severe that Mother Robinson moved the family to California, thus giving Jackie the opportunity to attend University of California Los Angeles (UCLA).

At UCLA Jackie demonstrated his prowess in football, baseball, basketball and the track and field. After serving as an officer in the US army during World War II, Jackie returned and began to emphasize baseball above the other sports that he could play. The decision made at this stage gave Robinson the opportunity to be the first black Major Leaguer in sixty years. In 1947, the Brooklyn Dodgers' president, Branch Rickey invited Jackie to join the Brooklyn Dodgers. No Major League team had had an African-American player since 1889, when baseball became segregated. Apart from being black, Jackie Robinson was 27 years old when he was invited to join the team. It was unusual for someone to make his major league debut at this age. Jackie became famous for not backing down when faced with the most difficult of circumstances. As a lieutenant in the army, he risked a court-martial by refusing to sit in the back of a military bus. In his first season with the Dodgers, the players made life difficult for Jackie. A group of Dodger players, led by Dixie Walker, suggested they would strike rather than play alongside Robinson. The team management told them that Jackie would play and that Dixie and his mates could leave if they wished. Robinson found solace in the company of Pittsburgh Pirate Hank Greenberg, the first major Jewish baseball star who had experienced anti-Semitic abuse.

Through persistence, Robinson was named Rookie of the year in 1947. He was named the league's most valuable player in 1949; after playing for eight more years, Robinson retired from baseball in 1957 and became a business executive with the NAACP . During his baseball years Jackie, in spite of the indignities heaped on him, he never gave them occasion to find fault with his attitude and behavior. He was an exceptionally talented and disciplined hitter, with a career average of .317. He was known as the most aggressive and successful base runner of his era. He consistently disrupted the concentration of pitchers, catchers and middle infielders. His home plate prowess and defensive skills allowed him to be regarded as one of the most intelligent baseball players of any era. It was almost impossible to get him as the last man out.

Most of Robinson's big challenges were off-field. In spite of his sterling performance on the field, his team mates signed a petition to get him off the team. Base runners' dug and kicked their spiked shoes into his shins. Substitutes on the bench wanted him to carry their bags and drinks. Fans of the Brooklyn Dodgers preferred that the team lose without Robinson than win with him on the team. However, of the 10 years that Robinson played baseball, 6 were spent leading the Brooklyn Dodgers into the World Series. His #42 jersey was retired by Major League Baseball in 1997. In 1962, he was inducted into baseball's Hall of Fame. He died at the premature age of 53 in 1972. After his death the Jackie Robinson Foundation was instituted to provide scholarships which help up to 141 students annually.

The most significant thing about Jackie Robinson is not only his personal dignity, but also his integrity of character. He has been spoken of as one of the most intelligent and persistent players to ever play baseball. His dignity challenged those around him to improve their talents, which says, in effect, he made a team out of those who did not even care for him. (With some modifications, the biography of Jackie Robinson was taken from Wikipedia).

> Life is not a spectator sport. If you're going to spend your whole life in the grandstand just watching what goes on, in my opinion, you're wasting your life.
>
> **- Jackie Robinson**

ACTIVITY I – Cheating and Lying

---

1. What do you think of the quote in the box on the previous page?

2. Below are some actions that suggest a baseball player has lost his/her head and compromised his/her dignity and integrity? Add to the list and explain how it might impact their dignity.

   a. Scuffing the ball

   b. Corking the bat

   c. Harassing the opponent

   d. Chewing tobacco

   e. Spitting in a dugout

   f. Betting on a game

   g. Using inappropriate language

   h. Using enhancement drugs (Steroids and Growth Hormones)

   i. Throwing a ball to hurt an opponent

   j. _____

   k. _____

   l. _____

3. How important do you think dignity and integrity are in your game of life?

ACTIVITY II – The use of language

---

1. Is it important to speak in a language that reflects your personal dignity?

   Yes ____ No ____ Do not know ____ Do not care ____

2. Do you have an understanding of what other people think about the kind of language you use?

   Yes ____ No ____ Do not know ____ Do not care ____

3. How much do you think positive or negative language affect your behavior?

   A lot ____ Not very much ____ Do not care ____

4. Reflect on how you speak now and state in what ways you need to improve your language game.

Explain_____

---

5. How do you think people's dress might affect the way that other people favor or scorn them?

_____

6. Is there any way to live without a mask and be comfortable?

_____

7. Stand before a mirror and look yourself in the eye then comment on how you feel about yourself?

_____

8. Stand before the mirror again and change the angle at which you first saw yourself, then describe how you feel at this point _____

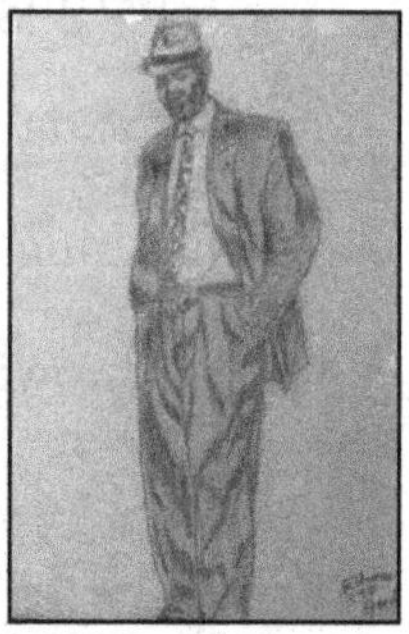

9. If you feel badly about yourself your dress profile, how might you change your feelings?

       a. Break the mirror _____

       b. Change you dress _____

       c. Transform yourself internally _____

10. From the actions above which would give you the best satisfaction? _____

Why?_____

11. Look at these two above pictures and say which seems more dignified to you? _____

12. Why have you made the choice you have? _____

13. How might your present appearance affect your opportunity for success?

_____

_____

14. Do you think your present appearance demonstrate respect for yourself? _____

15. Do you think your present appearance show respect for those about you? _____

16. Do you think your present appearance show respect for God? _____

17. How can your words affect people's perception of your dignity?

_____

18. How can the friends you choose impact your dignity?

_____

How might your dress affect your opportunity for success?

_____

_____

ACTIVITY IV – Thinking and doing

Read the statement below:

"One's dignity may be assaulted, vandalized and cruelly mocked, but it cannot be taken away unless it is surrendered." -Morton Kondrake

   a) Tell what you think of it.

_____

_____

_____

   b) How does it help you to think more carefully about your dignity and integrity?

_____

_____

_____

_____

_____

_____

B. Circle any word in the table below to describe your self-perception. Always = 8, Sometimes = 4 and Never = 2

	8	4	2
Acts constructively	Always	Sometimes	Never
Behaves non destructively	Always	Sometimes	Never
Consistent in actions	Always	Sometimes	Never
Distinguishes between good and bad actions	Always	Sometimes	Never
Expresses self with respect	Always	Sometimes	Never
Forgives others easily	Always	Sometimes	Never
Graceful and humble	Always	Sometimes	Never
Helpful to others	Always	Sometimes	Never
Immobilized by anger	Always	Sometimes	Never
Jettisons wrong judgment	Always	Sometimes	Never
Knows my obsessions	Always	Sometimes	Never
Learns the things that are important	Always	Sometimes	Never
Maintains a good sense of well-being	Always	Sometimes	Never
Nurtures that which is positive	Always	Sometimes	Never
Only open to that which is genuine	Always	Sometimes	Never

Perceptive of the good qualities of life	*Always*	Sometimes	*Never*
Quells indecency	*Always*	Sometimes	*Never*
Resist the negatives of life	*Always*	Sometimes	*Never*
Seeks wisdom to make the right decisions	*Always*	Sometimes	*Never*
Tenacious about that which is positive	*Always*	Sometimes	*Never*
Understands the consequences of wrong actions	Always	Sometimes	*Never*
Values truth	*Always*	Sometimes	*Never*
Wins graciously	*Always*	Sometimes	*Never*
Xeriscapes life – i.e. conserves	*Always*	Sometimes	*Never*
Yearns for uprightness	*Always*	Sometimes	*Never*
Zealously supports that which is worthy	*Always*	Sometimes	*Never*

Total the score and see how you fair. List all the adjustments you would wish to make with your life at this moment.

65-78 = You are doing very well

57-64 = You need to begin thinking about what adjustments are to be made

56 and below = You need to make serious adjustments

C. *What adjustments do you see yourself making in the near future?*

1. _____

2. _____

3. _____

Tips on making adjustments:

1. Help you to keep on track for success

2. Help you to access your progress in fulfilling your goals

3. Help you to avoid panic

4. Help you make improvements

5. Help you to become more accountability

6. Help you to overcome unhappiness

7. Help you with management

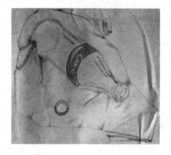

Activity IV: Behavior and character

A. What do you know of the following baseball players of other games? Share some experiences which may have brought them either to the hall of fame or a hall of shame?

NAME	CAREER	FAME	SHAME
PETE ROSE			
BARRY BONDS			
DARRYL STRAWBERRY			
DWIGHT GOODEN			
LENNY DYKSTRA			
SAMMY SOSA			
ROGER CLEMENTS			
TIGER WOODS			
MICHAEL VICK			

MARION JONES			
MARK MAGUIRE			
LEBRON JAMES			
KOBE BRYANT			
LAWRENCE TAYLOR			
DENNIS RODMAN			

B. Write a paragraph on the lines below about what you have learned from the names above about dignity and integrity. **You might mention such things as – drugs addictions, lying, drunk driving (DWI), sexual indiscretions, etc.**

_____

_____

_____

_____

_____

GOD'S MAP FOR YOUR DIGNITY AND INTEGRITY

Joseph: A Man of Dignity

Talk about dignity. This is a characteristic that was well seated in Joseph. All those around him could see it, but it was most transparent to Potiphar, the chief of Pharaoh's bodyguard, then to the prisoners and the chief jailer (Genesis 39), later to Pharaoh and the inhabitants of Egypt, and finally his brothers who eventually came to join him in Egypt (Genesis 40-50). Such dignity was evident in the way he deported himself among his fellow prisoners. Though not spelled out fully, a good evaluation does suggest that he must have earned the respect of the prisoners and the chief jailer by his demeanor and attitude. The biblical record makes clear that "the chief jailer committed to Joseph's charge all the prisoners who were in the jail; so that whatever was done there, he was responsible for it. The chief jailer did not supervise anything under Joseph's charge, because the Lord was with him; and whatever he did, the Lord made to prosper" (Genesis 39:22-33). More transparently, his dignity was expressed in the way he comported himself in Potiphar's house. As the chief steward, he had access to every part of the house and everything in it. However, it is clear that when Potipher's wife tried to proposition him, he did not yield. The record says,

> Now Joseph was well-built and handsome, and after a while his master's wife took notice of Joseph and said, "Come to bed with me!" But he refused. "With me in charge," he told her, "my master does not concern himself with anything in the house; everything he owns he has entrusted to my care. No one is greater in this house than I am. My master has withheld nothing from me except you, because you are his wife. How then could I do such a wicked thing and sin against God?" And though she spoke to Joseph day after day, he refused to go to bed with her or even be with her. One day he went into the house to attend to his duties, and none of the household servants was inside. She caught him by his cloak and said, "Come to bed with me!" But he left his cloak in her hand and ran out of the house. – Genesis 39:7-12.

Many points are suggested about Joseph's morality and spirituality, but the emphasis here is simply that Joseph respected his God, himself, his master, his mistress, and all those with whom he would associate. To Joseph, respect was a non–negotiable value. In regard to the issue of respect in sexual behavior, the Egyptian Governor Ptah-Hotep who ruled during the third dynasty says in his *Instruction*, "If you would be held in esteem in the house wherein you enter, whether it be that of a ruler, or of a brother, or of a friend, wherever you do enter, beware of approaching the wife, for it is not in any way a good thing to do. It is senseless. Thousands of men have destroyed themselves and gone to their deaths for the sake of the enjoyment of a pleasure which is as fleeting as the twinkling of an eye." - *Precept XVIII*. An extension of the point made states that respect gets respect. One who gives respect to others will normally receive due respect. One cannot go about disrespecting (dissing) others and then call for personal respect. Joseph showed respect and got a lot of it.

Since one of the areas of struggle in the urban culture of many youths today has to do with appearance, a little attention is being directed to dress. And there is no question as to whether Joseph dressed appropriately. From his youth it was made clear to him that he was to be a leader. His coat which was most carefully and colorfully woven and given to him by his father, said much about what was expected of him. Clothing speaks a lot, not only to others, but it also speaks to oneself who one is. The comment that Joseph was, "beautiful of form and fair to look upon," might have much to say concerning his personality, his physical condition, as well as the appearance of his dress. When he went to interpret the king's dream he changed his prison clothes. When he was promoted to be governor, his appearance (dress) was exquisite. The simple point here is that dress gives good expression to dignity or even helps to create it. This is why many groups wear their uniforms. They are making a statement about the dignity of appearance. Of course, clothing that is worn to hide the truth of one's negative character only makes dignity a sham. We must learn from Joseph that the right clothing and a dignified character will take us a far way.

> *So Pharaoh sent for Joseph, and he was quickly brought from the dungeon. When he had shaved and changed his clothes, he came before Pharaoh.*

How well do the following passages demonstrate the principles necessary for the development of dignity?

1. The value of reputation

Proverbs 22:1- *"A good name is more desirable than great riches; to be esteemed is better than silver or gold."*

2. The value of character

Proverbs 10:9- *"The man of integrity walks securely, but he who takes crooked paths will be found out."*

Proverbs 11:3- *"The integrity of the upright guides them, but the unfaithful are destroyed by their duplicity."*

On the Diamond of Dignity, look at yourself and see what help you might need.

YOU HAVE A HIGH
REGARD OF YOUR
SELF-WORTH

YOU HAVE A
POSITIVE SENSE OF
SELF-RESPECT

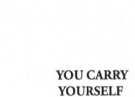

YOU CARRY
YOURSELF
WITH PRIDE

*Do you like what you have seen so far?
After you look back at the things you have seen concerning
your dignity, respond to the questions on the next page that
truly describe your personal dignity.*

TRANSFORMING YOUR ROAD MAP

1. Look carefully at yourself, then reflect on how well you see yourself displaying traits of dignity in your everyday life.

2. What do you see as the most desirable aspects of dignity?

3. Do you see yourself as a dignified person? Give insights to explain your response.

4. What are some skills you possess that are helpful in your development of being a dignified person?

5. What are some challenges that can negatively impact your effort to develop a dignified life?

6. What kinds of supports do you think are necessary to help in the development of your dignity?

Conclusion: The point of this discussion deals with the impact of personal dignity on success.

Sometimes we need to focus on the overt signals that we send to others about who we are.

The power of words affects the way that we are received.

Our behavior impacts the way that we are perceived.

How dignified are we?

DELIGHT

"Simplicity, clarity, singleness: these are the attributes that give our lives power and vividness and joy."

– Richard Halloway

LEARNING TO CELEBRATE YOUR LIFE

Baseball used to be known as "America's afternoon sports delight." Of course, with the development of television and the need for securing a larger audience, most of the afternoon delights have been shifted to the nights. However, with the expansive geography of America, the afternoon games, the Play-Offs and the World Series make the setting of the game time difficult for everyone across the country to share coordinated delightfulness from each game. However, that does not say that the game has lost the moments of delight.

Whether or not all are able to see the final game, it is interesting to watch the delight at the end

of a world series. On the day of
as the winning team is paraded
bands and the ticker tape parade
Fans and the winning team feel
opposite feelings quite often bring
have seen how the members of a
when they feel they have reached

There is no celebration without delight

celebration utter delight is seen,
through their city. The marching
all help to heighten the delight.
the sense of delight while the
disillusionment to the losers. We
losing team cry. They shed tears
a dead-end.

One can compare a baseball season to preparation for graduation. The preparation can be gruesome, but the day of graduation brings delight. During the preparation one imagines hearing "Pomp and Circumstance" being played. On the day of graduation, one does not mind what place one has in the marching line. When seated, each listens to the speeches that are given, but the crucial moment comes when names are called, shouts and screams, hoots, and hollers are heard, while tears of jubilation are shed as parchments are handed out. The graduate knows that a season or journey has come to a delightful end.

ACTIVITY I

A. Please answer the following questions.

1. Have you ever felt a profound sense of delight? Yes _____ No _____ Not sure _____

Describe

_____

_____

2. Which situation has brought you the greatest sense of delight?

_____

_____

_____

3. How have you celebrated your delight? (a) Drinking (b) Clubbing? (c) Displaying trophies? (d) Sharing photos on Facebook? (e) Celebrating at a worship service? (f) Inviting friends for dinner?

B. On a scale of 1-10 with 1 being the lowest and 10 being the highest, rate the following about how you feel about your sense of delight?

1.___ Satisfied		1.___Disappointed
2.___Gratified		2.___Depressed
3.___Vivacious		3.___Disgusted
4.___Thrilled		4.___Dissatisfied
5. ___Pleased		5. ___Displeased
6. ___Accomplished		6. ___Dejected
7. ___Excited		7. ___Distressed
8. ___Happy		8. ___Disillusioned
9. ___Contented		9. ___ Distraught
10. __Elated		10. __Disheartened

GOD'S MAP FOR YOUR DELIGHT

Joseph's "Sweet Revenge . . . ."

If one really wants to learn about delight, check with Joseph, who from our perspective was among the greatest governors of Egypt. His brothers hated him with a passion; that was good enough a reason to dissuade him from his destination. He was sold into Egyptian slavery; that was more reason to discourage him. He was put in prison, though thoroughly innocent of any crime; that was enough to destroy him. But, he was not dissuaded, discouraged, or destroyed. In the end, he became the second most powerful man in Egypt. He was given the authority to execute the plan that he had brought before Pharaoh when he interpreted Pharaoh's dream. Genesis 41 tells of some exciting things that took place as Joseph was promoted to the governorship of Egypt: (1) He was given Pharaoh's signet ring so that he could use Pharaoh's authority to enact laws concerning the administration of the kingdom. (2) He was dressed in a robe given to him by Pharaoh and provided with chariot for traveling over the kingdom. (3) He was lauded through the streets of Egypt as a sentinel called out his honor. (4) By the institution of his plans, he was able to gather an abundance of grain during the years of plenty; so much grain that he advised his work crew to stop measuring. (5) Pharaoh gave him the daughter of Potiphara the priest of On, to be his wife. He became the father of two sons. The first son was called Manasseh because he said, "God made me forget all my toil and my entire father's house." The second son was called Ephraim, which means "God made me fruitful in the land of my affliction." (6) When he was well established in the governorship, a turn of events caused him to meet his brothers and became reconciled to them. (7) He was also able to see his father again, and invited the whole family to live in Egypt.

The points of emphases are:

(1)   Joseph was avenged.

(2)   Joseph overcame his prideful weaknesses that had gotten him in trouble in the first place with his brothers.

(3)   Joseph was promoted to his place of destiny, to which God had intended. God was guiding him through all the times of struggles and troubles.

(4)   Joseph was reconciled to his family.

(5)   Joseph was filled with delight. His joys knew no bound.

Just envision Joseph sitting at his first meal with his brothers as part of the reconciliation. Although he did not sit at the same table, his heart was filled with delight. Even when he was evaluating his brothers to see how much they had overcome their meanness, he was focused on delight rather than revenge. He was not thinking now of the days of his suffering, but instead, he felt a profound sense of delight when he said to his brothers:

> "I am Joseph! Is my father still living?" But his brothers were not able to answer him, because they were terrified at his presence. Then Joseph said to his brothers, "Come close to me." When they had done so, he said, "I am your brother Joseph, the one you sold into Egypt! And now, do not be distressed and do not be angry with yourselves for selling me here, because it was to save lives that God sent me ahead of you. For two years now there has been famine in the land, and for the next five years there will not be plowing and reaping. [7] But God sent me ahead of you to preserve for you a remnant on earth and to save your lives by a great deliverance. "So then, it was not you who sent me here, but God. He made me father to Pharaoh, lord of his entire household and ruler of all Egypt." (Genesis 45:3-8).

The delight of Jacob should also be noted. When he met with Joseph, he saw how his parental desire for his son's success had come true. Was he therefore filled with delight? Sure! Many commentators have emphasized the favoritism with which Jacob treated Joseph, but a positive interpretation can be seen when we come to realize that all good parents wish the best for their children. Thus when Jacob met Joseph as the Governor of Egypt, his heart was filled with nothing but delight.

Below are some scriptural passages that give important insights about delight, read them and see how they impact you.

1. Working with delight

*Proverbs 8:30 Then I was the craftsman at his side. I was filled with **delight** day after day, rejoicing always in his presence*

2. The delight of the fool

*Proverbs 10:23 A fool finds pleasure in evil conduct, but a man of understanding **delight**s in wisdom.*

*Proverbs 11:20 The Lord detests men of perverse heart but he **delights** in those whose ways are blameless.*

The delight of the wise

Psalm 37:4 Delight yourself in the Lord and he will give you the desires of your heart.

On the Diamond of Delight, look at yourself to see what help you might need.

ARE YOU EXCITED
WITH WHAT YOU
HAVE ACHIEVED IN
LIFE?

DO YOU FEEL
FULFILLED
AS YOU RUN
THE BASES OF
LIFE?

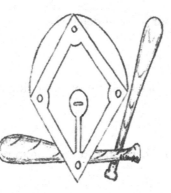

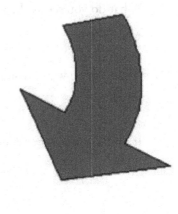

ARE YOU SATISFIED
TO BE ON HOME
BASE?

Do you like what you have seen?
After you look back at your focus and management of your
delight, respond to the questions on the next page that truly
describe your delights.

TRANSFORMING YOUR ROAD MAP

1. Describe your sense of delight as you came to the end of any journey that you have taken.

2. How long did you maintain your sense of delight?

3. What do you see as the greatest deterrent to your enjoying the delights of your life?

4. What advice would you give to others who are seeking to reach a sense of sustained delight?

5. If you are not experiencing times of delight in your life today, what changes do you wish to make?

6. What kind of support might you need to help you achieve a better level of delight, than you now have?

> *"If you do not smile at success, success will always smile at you."*
>
> *-Lao Tzu*

ASSESSING YOUR PERSONAL COMMITMENTS

On a scale of 1 to 5 (with 1 being the lowest) rate yourself in the following categories:

I am a visionary	1	2	3	4	5
I think positively most of the time	1	2	3	4	5
I arrive at my appointments on time	1	2	3	4	5
I take initiative at all times	1	2	3	4	5
I am an energetic leader	1	2	3	4	5
I am a team player	1	2	3	4	5
I am very focused and disciplined	1	2	3	4	5
I am an organized person	1	2	3	4	5
I am a detailed oriented person	1	2	3	4	5
I am very focused on excellence	1	2	3	4	5
I am a creative person	1	2	3	4	5
I am generally dressed well and appropriately	1	2	3	4	5
I am a decisive person	1	2	3	4	5
I am a dependable person	1	2	3	4	5
I work effectively with others	1	2	3	4	5
I am an ambitious person	1	2	3	4	5
I am a goal oriented person	1	2	3	4	5
I am a strategic thinking person	1	2	3	4	5
I am helpful to others around me	1	2	3	4	5
I am a very respectful person	1	2	3	4	5
Totals					

Add up the columns and state how you feel about your rating?

If you get 90-100 you are highly committed.

If you got 80-90 you are quite committed.

If you get 65-80 you are committed.

Below 65 you need to work on your level of commitment.

What changes do you wish to make in order to reach a more delightful life? _____

Name two areas that you wish to change in order to be more effective in taking charge of your desired life by adding words to complete the thoughts.

1. I will _____ to live a more positive life and to reach my destination.

2. I will _____ to live a more positive life and to reach my destination.

If you desire to seal your commitment for a successful journey, complete and sign the pledge below

Before God and humanity I _____ pledge to live up to the path of my life which God has chosen for me.

I will seek to focus on a clear purpose, make positive decisions, being serious with my dedication, determination, diligence, discernment, and practice integrity in all my relations.

I will seek the aid of a positive role model/coach to help guide me to my destination.

Signed _____ Date _____

Celebrating your life

If you have ever enjoyed delightful times in your life's journey, praise God for such moments. When Joseph ate his unity meal with his brothers, he gave praise to God for his journey of life (cf. Genesis 45:1-6).

In looking back at his life, after his many days in baseball, Jackie Robinson was able to say, "The way I figured it, I was even with baseball and baseball with me. The game had done much for me, and I had done much for it." Mark Twain said, "Twenty years from now you will be more disappointed by the things that you didn't do than by the ones you did do. So throw off the bowlines. Sail away from the safe harbour. Catch the trade winds in your sails. Explore. Dream. Discover."

George Clooney, quoting his father, said, "Whatever you do, don't wake up at 65 years old and think about what you should have done with your life."

Celebrating your mentors

No successful destination is ever reached without family, friends, teachers, coaches and managers, etc, so it is also time to have a party for those who have helped you.

Send a card to a person who has helped you to reach where you are in life.

Send some flowers. Invite a friend who has been kind to you to a World Series game or a Super Bowl party. You might be surprised that you have given that friend a delightful day.

Celebrating your second chance

Never forget that life has given you many opportunities to turn your situation around. Thank God for second chances. Life comes with no guarantees, so accept the frustrations, disappointments, heartbreaks, failures, but don't let them hold you back. Dream what you need to dream. Be what you want to be. Don't be afraid to take risks. Learn to live life to the fullest.

LEARN TO INCLUDE GOD IN EVERY ASPECT OF YOUR LIFE FOR IT IS GOD WHO BRINGS US DELIGHT

You might pray what Cardinal Richard Cushing prayed many years ago for a game in Chicago.

DEAR GOD,

Help me be a good sport in the game of life. I don't ask for an easy place in the lineup. Put me anywhere you need me. I only ask that I can give you 100% of everything I have. If all the hard drives seem to come my way, I thank you for the compliment. Help me to remember that you never send a player more trouble than he can handle with your help…

And help me, Lord, to accept the bad breaks as part of the game. May I always play on the square no matter what others do…Help me study…THE BOOK so I'll know the rules. . .

Finally, God, if the natural turns of events go against me and I am benched for sickness or old age, help me accept that as a part of the game, too. Keep me from whimpering that I was framed or that I got a raw deal. And when I finish the final inning, I ask for no laurels; all I want is to believe in my heart, I played as well as I could and that I didn't let you down.

Amen.

Or you might choose to pray your own words. We should always to keep in mind that "We are not the measure of all things." We need God in the Pit, as on the Bases and when we reach Home-Base we are to thank God for reaching. A persons God is anything that is in first place in their life. Ask yourself who is or what is my god?

Conclusion: At every stage of our lives' journey, we are to take time to celebrate our progression.

We are to give a thank you party for family and friends who have supported us along the way.

We are to celebrate by praising God for making it possible for us to succeed in whatever we dream.

Life is full of delights. Learn to appreciate the delightful moments.

Where is your reality?

It all about perspective

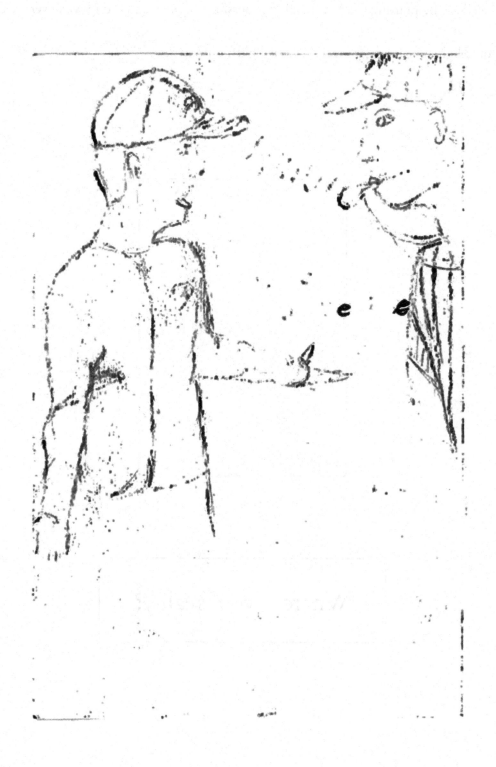

DURATIVE (OR LASTING) LEGACY

EVERY LIFE HAS A LEGACY: HALL OF FAME OR HALL OF SHAME

Thinking through what we have sought to accomplish in life is the best way to evaluate how successful we have been. It is an unfortunate thing that many persons never access their lives by asking themselves critical questions about the extent of their failures or successes. Why did they fail? Why did they succeed where/when they succeeded? Some people prefer to live their lives in ignorance. They do not want to know the reasons for their failures or successes, in which case, they will never grow.

Another aspect of life concerning which we need to ask questions is that of legacies. What are our legacies? How do we want to leave life? What would we like people to say about us at our funerals? How well did we follow the rules of life? How well did we play our part in the game? How did we deal with the obstacles, frustrations, heart-breaks that confronted us? What particular corrections did we make as we played the game? Did we achieve the end that we set forth for the game? How much delight did we experience when the game was being played and when it was over? How much frustration or disillusionment are we still experiencing after the game is over? These are critical questions for anyone who has played the game of life.

One either ends the game of life in a Hall of Fame or a Hall of Shame. In speaking thus we are using baseball or basketball language, but life runs a course that ends in one of these two directions. Getting in the Hall of Fame is tricky business these days for people are pumped on steroids. Those who vote people in are having a hard time for many who are nominated reputations are very soiled. Those who understand the seriousness of playing the game of life have argued that it is not about numbers or statistics but about character. How does one get to the Hall of Fame? By lying, by cheating, by gambling, or by drugging? We are speaking in mundane terms for in the end, we know that that Hall of Fame or the Hall of Shame is not for human beings to decide. In which case we either choose to do that which will be acceptable to God and be in God's Hall of Fame or we might do any of the things that cheaters and liars like to do and get into the Hall of Shame.

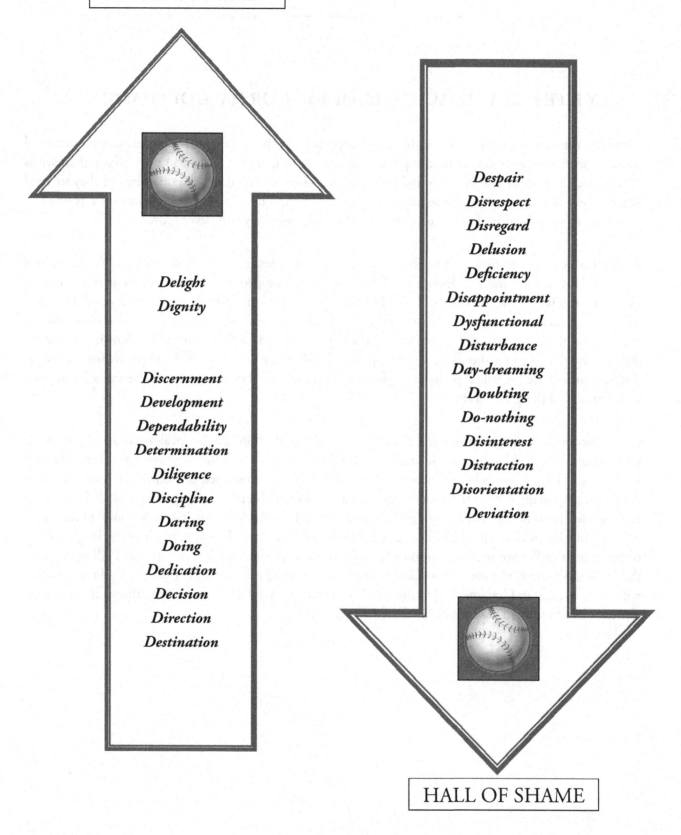

HALL OF FAME

Delight
Dignity

Discernment
Development
Dependability
Determination
Diligence
Discipline
Daring
Doing
Dedication
Decision
Direction
Destination

Despair
Disrespect
Disregard
Delusion
Deficiency
Disappointment
Dysfunctional
Disturbance
Day-dreaming
Doubting
Do-nothing
Disinterest
Distraction
Disorientation
Deviation

HALL OF SHAME

If one reaches the Hall of Fame then he/she can rest. But to reach the Hall of Fame is not to be considered our ultimate destiny. Thus one needs to ask, before one rests, what is my ultimate destiny? Is it just to be successful in the world's Halls of Fame? Is it to be rich or drive a luxury car, living in a big house, having a family or what? It is clear that no one truly finds total happiness in any aspect of this life until one finds the true source of meaning in God? We need not do a lot of God talk here, but we need to note that just about every human being can resonate with the great philosopher and Theologian Augustine of Hippo who lived a rather reckless life in his youth but found that he was not able to satisfy his restlessness until he connected himself to the Greatest source of Meaning. In his *Confessions* he said, "My heart had not rest until it found rest in Thee." In effect, while we have put forth multiple steps for a successful destination, we should know that if we do not center our lives in God's Hall of Fame, then we shall enter the devil's Hall of Shame. In the former hall there is celebration, in the latter hall there is desperation and despair.

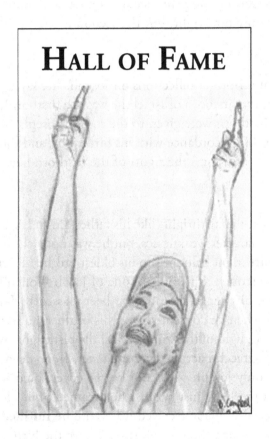

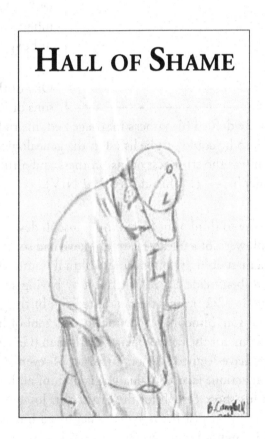

THE CHOICE IS YOURS!!!

SPIRITUAL VALUES THAT REFLECT ON OUR FINAL DESTINATION

In looking at the many lives we have pursued, none stand out so clear as the life of Joseph. His is the most worthy of emulation. He distinguished himself as a dreamer and leader and at the end of his life he entered a Hall of Fame rather than a Hall of Shame. Things could have been much different if he would have allowed himself to be dissuaded, distracted, and diverted, but he followed a straight path that led to his successful destiny. When he was tempted to fulfill immediate self-gratifications he cried out, "How can I do this wicked thing and sin against my God." (Genesis 39:9). He was loyal to himself, his master and his God. He had made certain personal commitments that he was not willing to trade for anything immediate and thus he not only inherited the family birthright, but the second highest position in Egypt.

One of the great scriptural reflections on Joseph's life says, "The sons of Reuben, the firstborn of Israel (he was the firstborn), but when he defiled his father's marriage bed, his rights as firstborn were given to the sons of Joseph, son of Israel; so he could not be listed in the genealogical record in accordance with his birthright, and though Judah was the strongest of his brothers and a ruler came from him, the rights of the firstborn belonged to Joseph." — (1 Chronicles 5:1, 2 NIV).

It is easy to think that in dreaming Joseph desired to cheat the birthright, like his father did to Esau, but Joseph was not a cheat. He might have had some other character weaknesses, but he was not a cheat. He was a man of high honor. In his cultural tradition, the birthright belonged to his oldest brother, Rueben. But Ruben made a fool of himself by having sexual intercourse with Bilhah, one of Jacob's concubines (Genesis 32:22), and thus forfeited the birthright. The birthright should have been passed to Jacob's second son, Simeon, but he too made a fool of himself when he consented with his brothers to murder Shechem, for the rape of their sister Dinah (Genesis 34). In light of this, Simeon lost the birthright. What might have seemed like a rightful act of revenge for a disgraceful action against a sister, Jacob deemed a rotten action. Jacob's evaluation is that, of all his sons, only Joseph could not keep a covenanted word. He thus chose Joseph for the birthright. Joseph did not receive it just because he dreamed of it. He did not receive it just because his father loved him in a special way. He received it because **he fulfilled the requirements for it**. When at the end of his life Jacob revealed that Joseph should have the birthright, Joseph had already been honored in his family and honored in Egypt. He took the precedence, gaining privileges that the brothers never obtained. In fact, when the children of Israel resettled in the Promised Land, ten of the tribes carried the name of Ephraim, Joseph's youngest son. Only the tribe of Judah received an equal or greater honor, as the tribe from which David and the Messiah came.

Yes, through the life of Joseph we have learned that individuals might have great dreams, but dreaming alone is not assurance of winning the game of life. There is a need for discovering who one is. There is also need for having a clear sense of direction, learning how to make proper decisions, understanding the need for dedication, determination and discipline. One might face many adversities; dreams and visions might seem broken, but dreams and visions can be repaired if one maintains a firm focus on life and seeks what God wants to do with and through them. The problem with too many folks who want to be great or successful is that they leave God out of their lives. A thought that was taken from a card we purchased some time ago is very inspiring in this vein:

Always remember,

When you walk with the Lord, He will guide you.

When you run, He will sustain you.

When you fly, yes, when you fly

He will take you places you never dreamed.

Taken from Courageous Movie

APPENDICES

APPENDIX I – A SAMPLE PERSONALITY TEST APPENIX - A

Sanguine

- The Sanguine temperament personality is fairly extroverted. People of a sanguine temperament tend to enjoy social gatherings, making new friends and tend to be quite loud. They are usually quite creative and often daydream. However, some alone time is crucial for those of this temperament. Sanguine can also mean very sensitive, compassionate and thoughtful. Sanguine personalities generally struggle with following tasks all the way through, are chronically late, and tend to be forgetful and sometimes a little sarcastic. Often, when pursuing a new hobby, interest is lost quickly when it ceases to be engaging or fun. They are very much people persons. They are talkative and not shy. For some people, these are the ones you want to be friends with and usually they become life-long friends.

Choleric

- A person who is choleric is a do-er. Such a person has a lot of ambition, energy, and passion, and tries to instill it in others. Such a person can dominate people of other temperaments, especially phlegmatic types. Many great charismatic military and political figures have been cholerics. They like to be leaders and in charge of everything.

Melancholic

- A person who is a thoughtful ponderer has a *melancholic* disposition. Often very considerate and get rather worried when he could not be on time for events? melancholics can be highly creative in activities such as poetry and art - and can become occupied with the tragedy and cruelty in the world. *Melancholic*s are also often a perfectionist. They are often self-reliant and independent; one negative part of being a melancholic is sometimes they can get so involved in what they are doing that they forget to think of others.

Phlegmatic

- Phlegmatics tend to be self-content and kind. They can be very accepting and affectionate. They may be very receptive and shy and often prefer stability to uncertainty and change. They are very consistent, relaxed, rational, curious, and observant, making them good administrators and astronauts.

Take the following sample Personality Test to see with which of the descriptions above you are most closely aligned.

1. You are almost never late for your appointments.
   ☐ YES ☐ NO

2. You like to be engaged in an active and fast-paced job.
   ☐ YES ☐ NO

3. You enjoy having a wide circle of acquaintances.
   ☐ YES ☐ NO

4. You feel involved when watching T.V. soaps.
   ☐ YES ☐ NO

5. You are usually the first to react to a sudden event: the telephone ringing or unexpected question.
   ☐ YES ☐ NO

6. You are interested in a general idea than in the details of its realization.
   ☐ YES ☐ NO

7. You tend to be unbiased even if this might endanger your good relations with people.
   ☐ YES ☐ NO

8. Strict observance of the established rules is likely to prevent a good outcome.
   ☐ YES ☐ NO

9. It's difficult to get you excited.
   ☐ YES ☐ NO

10. It is in your nature to assume responsibility.
    ☐ YES ☐ NO

11. You often think about humankind and its destiny.
    ☐ YES ☐ NO

12. You believe the best decision is one that can be easily changed.
    ☐ YES ☐ NO

13. Objective criticism is always useful in any activity.
    ☐ YES ☐ NO

14. You prefer to act immediately rather than speculate about various options.
    ☐ YES ☐ NO

15. You trust reason rather than feelings.
    ☐ YES ☐ NO

16. You are inclined to rely more on improvisation than on carefully planning.
☐ YES ☐ NO

17. You spend your leisure time actively socializing with a group of people, attending parties, shopping, etc.
☐ YES ☐ NO

18. You usually plan your actions in advance.
☐ YES ☐ NO

19. Your actions are frequently influenced by emotions.
☐ YES ☐ NO

20. You are a person somewhat reserved and distant in communication.
☐ YES ☐ NO

21. You know how to put every minute of your time to good purpose.
☐ YES ☐ NO

22. You readily help people while asking nothing in return.
☐ YES ☐ NO

23. You often contemplate about the complexity of life.
☐ YES ☐ NO

24. After prolonged socializing you feel you need to get away and be alone.
☐ YES ☐ NO

25. You often do jobs in a hurry.
☐ YES ☐ NO

26. You easily see the general principle behind specific occurrences.
☐ YES ☐ NO

27. You frequently and easily express your feelings and emotions.
☐ YES ☐ NO

28. You find it difficult to speak loudly.
☐ YES ☐ NO

29. You get bored if you have to read theoretical books.
☐ YES   ☐ NO

30. You tend to sympathize with other people.
☐ YES   ☐ NO

31. You value justice higher than mercy.
☐ YES   ☐ NO

32. You rapidly get involved in social life at a new workplace.
☐ YES   ☐ NO

33. The more people with whom you speak, the better you feel.
☐ YES   ☐ NO

34. You tend to rely on your experience rather than on theoretical alternatives.
☐ YES   ☐ NO

35. You like to keep a check on how things are progressing.
☐ YES   ☐ NO

36. You easily empathize with the concerns of other people.
☐ YES   ☐ NO

37. Often you prefer to read a book than go to a party.
☐ YES   ☐ NO

38. You enjoy being at the center of events in which other people are directly involved.
☐ YES   ☐ NO

39. You are more inclined to experiment than to follow familiar approaches.
☐ YES   ☐ NO

40. You avoid being bound by obligations.
☐ YES   ☐ NO

41. Your are strongly touched by the stories about people's troubles.
☐ YES   ☐ NO

42. Deadlines seem to you to be of relative, rather than absolute, importance.
☐ YES   ☐ NO

43. You prefer to isolate yourself from outside noises.
☐ YES   ☐ NO

44. It's essential for you to try things with your own hands.
☐ YES   ☐ NO

45. You think that almost everything can be analyzed.
☐ YES ☐ NO

46. You do your best to complete a task on time.
☐ YES ☐ NO

47. You take pleasure in putting things in order.
☐ YES ☐ NO

48. You feel at ease in a crowd.
☐ YES ☐ NO

49. You have good control over your desires and temptations.
☐ YES ☐ NO

50. You easily understand new theoretical principles.
☐ YES ☐ NO

51. The process of searching for solution is more important to you than the solution itself .
☐ YES ☐ NO

52. You usually place yourself nearer to the side than in the center of the room.
☐ YES ☐ NO

53. When solving a problem, you would rather follow a familiar approach than seek a new one.
☐ YES ☐ NO

54. You try to stand firmly by your principles.
☐ YES ☐ NO

55. A thirst for adventure is close to your heart.
☐ YES ☐ NO

56. You prefer meeting in small groups to interaction with lots of people.
☐ YES ☐ NO

57. When considering a situation you pay more attention to the current situation and less to a possible sequence of events.
☐ YES ☐ NO

58. You consider the scientific approach to be the best.
  ☐ YES ☐ NO

59. You find it difficult to talk about your feelings.
  ☐ YES ☐ NO

60. You often spend time thinking of how things could be improved.
  ☐ YES ☐ NO

61. Your decisions are based more on the feelings of a moment than on careful planning.
  ☐ YES ☐ NO

62. You prefer to spend your leisure time alone or relaxing in a tranquil family atmosphere.
  ☐ YES ☐ NO

63. You feel more comfortable sticking to conventional ways.
  ☐ YES ☐ NO

64. You are easily affected by strong emotions.
  ☐ YES ☐ NO

65. You are always looking for opportunities.
  ☐ YES ☐ NO

66. Your desk, workbench, etc. is usually neat and orderly.
  ☐ YES ☐ NO

67. As a rule, current preoccupations worry you more than your future plans.
  ☐ YES ☐ NO

68. You get pleasure from solitary walks.
  ☐ YES ☐ NO

69. It is easy for you to communicate in social situations.
  ☐ YES ☐ NO

70. You are consistent in your habits.
  ☐ YES ☐ NO

71. You willing involve yourself in matters which engage your sympathies.
  ☐ YES ☐ NO

72. You easily perceive various ways in which events could develop.
  ☐ YES ☐ NO

What is your personality?

Based on what you have read and checked above:

1. Can you tell what kind of personality you are? _____

2. Write a brief description of yourself. _____

_____

_____

_____

3. What are other people saying about your personality? _____

_____

_____

APPENDIX II – A SAMPLE TALENT TEST

TALENT ASSESSMENT

Talent assessment focuses on a person's skills and growth potential. It provides an opportunity for a quick and easy way to assess a person for personal and organizational development. A talent assessment is an in-depth review of a person's life history, patterns of behavior, accomplishments, areas for improvement, and projected growth. In one way a talent assessment might relate to a particular task, however the talent is not born because of that task. The talent is ability, which a person has and can be observed at any stage of a person's life. An assessment thus provides key insights and valuable information through the talent in relation to a certain task. At the conclusion of a talent assessment the results are used for managing, coaching, counseling, placement, planning, decision making and training of a person. The more a person has the opportunity to develop along the line of the talent, the more competent the person can be in life. A talent assessment will ask questions as indicated in the inventory below:

Some Inventory Questions	Very Poor	Poor	Fair	Average	Good	Very Good	Excellent	Out-standing
How focused?								
How flexible?								
How is your sight?								
How cautious?								
How relational?								
How physically strong?								
How mentally alert?								
How visionary?								
How persistent?								
How decisive?								
How confident?								
How communi-cative?								
How is your memory?								
How responsive?								
How agile?								
How are your listening skills?								
How well do you use your hands?								

How good are your feet?							
How reliable?							
Physically fit?							
How well do you run?							
How well do you walk?							

B. EVALUATE

As you take a look at your talents, what do you see as your strengths?

What are your challenges for what you desire to be?

What should you be selecting as a professional or career path?

APPENDIX III

A SAMPLE SPIRITUAL INVENTORY

Instructions:

For each of the 60 questions which follow, circle the number that corresponds with the response that most closely matches how you perceive yourself. Categories are presented diagonally, across the top of the inventory.

- 4, consistently true

- 3, frequently true

- 2, occasionally true

- 1, infrequently true

- 0, rarely true

You might also ask a person who is close to you to score the inventory with, and for, you. Their perception of your strengths may be useful in identifying the gifts with which you have been truly blessed. After responding to each question, turn to the scoring grid on page six to analyze your results.

1. When presented a goal, I immediately think of steps that need to be taken in order to achieve the desired results. 4 3 2 1 0

2. I express myself through artistic means. 4 3 2 1 0

3. My faith requires me to seek out God's will and purpose in all circumstances that arise in my life. 4 3 2 1 0

4. I am able to convey the Gospel message to non-believers in ways that they are able to easily understand. 4 3 2 1 0

5. I am moved by those who through conflict or sorrow are wavering in faith. 4 3 2 1 0

6. I am certain of the spirit's presence in my life and the lives of others. 4 3 2 1 0

7. I am blessed by God each day and gladly respond to these blessings by giving liberally of my time and money. 4 3 2 1 0

8. I enjoy meeting new people and becoming acquainted with them. 4 3 2 1 0

9. I know that God hears and responds to my daily prayers. 4 3 2 1 0

10. I feel compelled to learn as much as I can about the Bible and faith. 4 3 2 1 0

11. I am a take charge person. When others follow my direction, the goal or task will be completed. 4 3 2 1 0

12. When I see a person in need, I am moved to assist them. 4 3 2 1 0

13. I love to sing and enjoy inspiring others through song. 4 3 2 1 0

14. I find joy and express myself by playing a musical instrument. 4 3 2 1 0

15. I am motivated to provide spiritual leadership to those who are on a faith journey. 4 3 2 1 0

16. I like working behind the scenes to ensure projects are successful. 4 3 2 1 0

17. I enjoy working with my hands in a trade or skill that requires considerable experience to perfect. 4 3 2 1 0

18. My great joy is to communicate biblical truth in such a way that it becomes real and understood by others. 4 3 2 1 0

19. When a challenge is presented, I am usually able to identify an appropriate solution. 4 3 2 1 0

20. I am able to take a thought or idea and put it into a clear and inspiring written form. 4 3 2 1 0

21. I enjoy organizing thoughts, ideas, hopes and dreams into a specific plan of action. 4 3 2 1 0

22. I can translate into artistic form what I first see in my imagination. 4 3 2 1 0

23. I have assisted others as they sought to discern whether or not their personal decisions were helpful and in accord with God's will for their lives. 4 3 2 1 0

24. I enjoy being with non-believers and like having the opportunity to encourage them to faith and commitment. 4 3 2 1 0

25. When I know someone is facing a crisis, I feel compelled to provide support and care. 4 3 2 1 0

26. My trust in the Spirit's presence, when I encounter times of personal crisis, is a source of strength for others. 4 3 2 1

27. I manage my time and money so that I am able to give much of it to the work of the church or other organizations. 4 3 2 1 0

28. I am often asked to open my home for small group gatherings or social occasions.   4 3 2 1 0

29. I often become so absorbed in my prayer life that the door bell or phone can ring and I will not hear it. 4 3 2 1 0

30. Not one day would be complete without biblical study and thought. 4 3 2 1 0

31. When I am in a group, others will often look to me for direction. 4 3 2 1 0

32. I feel an urgency to provide housing for the homeless, food for the starving, comfort for those in distress. 4 3 2 1 0

33. I have sung before groups and felt a real sense of God's presence. 4 3 2 1 0

34. By my playing a musical instrument, inspiration has been provided for both myself and others. 4 3 2 1 0

35. I have responsibility for providing spiritual guidance to an individual believer or group of believers. 4 3 2 1 0

36. People tell me that without my willingness to do the unnoticed jobs, their work would be more difficult. 4 3 2 1 0

37. I am good at building, repairing, or restoring things and find satisfaction in doing so. 4 3 2 1 0

38. I want to express my faith by assisting others to discover the truths contained in the Bible. 4 3 2 1 0

39. People come to me for help in applying Christian faith and values to personal situations. 4 3 2 1 0

40. I often feel moved to write about my thoughts and feelings so others may benefit from them. 4 3 2 1 0

41. I have been successful in organizing, directing and motivating people to achieve a goal. 4 3 2 1 0

42. My artistic work has given spiritual strength to both believer and non-believer.   4 3 2 1 0

43. In the congregation, I am often asked if a direction being discussed is in accord with God's will and purpose. 4 3 2 1 0

44. I do not find it difficult to share what Jesus means to me with non-believers. 4 3 2 1 0

45. Those who are struggling with life questions have come to me for guidance and help. 4 3 2 1 0

46. I can see great things happening in my congregation and am not derailed by the pessimism of others. 4 3 2 1 0

47. When I receive money unexpectedly, one of my first thoughts is to share this gift through the church. 4 3 2 1 0

48. I enjoy welcoming guests and helping them to feel at ease. 4 3 2 1 0

49. Believers have asked me to pray for healing in their lives, and have evidenced God's healing power. 4 3 2 1 0

50. My study of the Bible has proven helpful to others in their faith journey. 4 3 2 1 0

51. People have said they like to work with me because the task will be successfully completed. 4 3 2 1 0

52. People have been surprised by how at ease I am while working with those who are suffering in mind, body or spirit. 4 3 2 1 0

53. I am grateful and humbled that my singing has provided inspiration and hope for others on their faith journey. 4 3 2 1 0

54. Others have told me they were moved by my playing a musical instrument. 4 3 2 1 0

55. People have come to me for spiritual help and it has developed into a long-term relationship. 4 3 2 1 0

56. When I turn out the lights, take tables down, work in the kitchen or put chairs away, I feel that I have served the Lord. 4 3 2 1 0

57. My knowledge of building, maintenance or repair has been a special value to the church and others. 4 3 2 1 0

58. Students have told me that I can take the most difficult idea or concept and make it understandable. 4 3 2 1 0

59. When direction is needed at work or in the congregation, I am generally asked for my opinion. 4 3 2 1 0

60. My written work has been helpful to others in understanding life's truths. 4 3 2 1 0

SCORING GRID:

For each set of three questions, fill in the number 0 1 2 3 4 5 6 7 8 9 10 11 12 of rectangular blocks equal to your total score. For example, in the category of Administration, the numbers 2+4+3 total 9. Once completed, note that the longer the bar the stronger the corresponding gift.

The strongest gift(s) will generally have a total score of "7" or more. If you have more than one gift with a total of seven or more, then all of these gifts can be referred to as your "gift cluster." Notice how each gift within the cluster has the potential to compliment and support another. The gifts within the cluster will need to be further explored to determine which ones you have truly been blessed with.

This inventory is designed to begin your journey toward spiritual gifts discovery. Keep in mind that it is not a scientific instrument. Your perceptions will be validated by others and confirmed through prayer and by their use over time. Identify your spiritual gift cluster, and then list the gifts in the gifts cluster.

0 1 2 3 4 5 6 7 8 9 10 11 12

Very likely you have a gift that does not appear in the list below, please add it if you think God has given it to you.

Administration (Management) Questions 1, 21, 41	**Art** **(Artistry)** Questions 2, 22, 42	**Discernment** (Wisdom) Questions 3, 23, 43
Evangelism **(Witnessing)** Questions 4, 24, 44	**Exhortation** (Encouragement) Questions 5, 25, 45	**Faith** (Faithfulness) Questions 6, 26, 46

Giving **(Stewardship)** Questions 7, 27, 47	**Hospitality** (Blessing strangers) Questions 8, 28, 48	**Intercession** Questions 9, 29, 49
Knowledge Questions 10, 30, 50	**Leadership** (Influencing) Questions 11, 31, 51	**Works of Mercy** (Working with the poor, sick and those who are incarcerated) Questions 12, 32, 52
Music Questions 13, 33, 53	**Praise Giving** Questions 14, 34, 54	**Shepherding (pastoring)** Questions 15, 35, 55
Service Questions 16, 36, 56	**Craft** Questions 17, 37, 57	**Teaching** Questions 18, 38, 58

Wisdom Questions 19, 39, 59	**Writing** Questions 20, 40, 60	**Miracles** (Health and Healing)
Help	**Exorcism** (Casting out demons)	**Speech** (Tongues and the Interpretation of Tongues)
Missionary (Planting Churches)	**Marriage** (Family)	**Celibacy** (Singleness)
Justice (At the heart of the gospel)	**Love** (The soul of every gift)	**CHRIST** (The ultimate gift)

Please focus on the fact that:

Your gifts are for your spiritual growth

Your gifts are not for self-gratification (or not for self-aggrandizement)

Your gifts are to help you build up others – to add to other people's happiness

Your gifts are to help you build a team – Success is greatest when people work together

Your gifts are to help you build up a community – the world is too isolated

Your gifts are to help you share good news about God

If other human beings are not blessed, your gifts are of no significant value

SOURCES TO HELP CLARIFY YOUR GAME PLAN

I. Brian Tracy, *Eat That Frog: 21 Great Ways to Stop Procrastinating & Get More Done in Less Time*, has a great summary of ideas on:

1. The ability to concentrate single-mindedly on your most important task, to do it well and to finish it completely, is the key to great success, achievement, respect, status and happiness in life.

2. The three key qualities to develop the habits of focus and concentration. These three qualities are decision, disciplineand determination.

3. The very worst use of time, namely doing something very well that need not be done at all.

4. The goals that are the fuel in the furnace of achievement.

5. How the weakest key result area can set the height at which you can use all your other skills and abilities.

6. How continuous learning is the minimum requirement for success in any field.

7. How, while making a yard might be hard; but inch by inch, anything is a cinch!

8. How difficulties come not to obstruct, but to instruct.

9. Why you can only get your time and your life under control to the degree to which you discontinue lower value activities.

II. Malcolm Gladwell, *Outliers: The Story of Success.*

This is a very powerful book about what makes for a successful life. Its thesis is that that makes a difference in the lives of people is that which stands outside the usually accepted rule of the game, that which is outside the generally accepted standard of life. As Gladwell defines it, it is "Something that is situated away from or classed differently from a main or related body." For him:

1. Ability needs Opportunity

2. Opportunity must be accompanied by hard work – the 10,000 –hour rule

3. Even geniuses must have opportunity and work hard and long

4. There must also be an accumulation of advantages - cultural (class) advantage to learn certain skills

5. Timing is also of great importance – If you are on time opportunities are open

6. There is also the need for courage to take risks.

7. The role that ambition plays

8. The kind of school that one attends

9. The involvement of parents in one's venture

10. The connections that one might have

11. The powerful forces that might impact the circumstances of one's life

12. The spirit of determination that one possesses to finish a job

13. The power of endurance

III. Joe Gibbs with Jerry B. Jenkins, *Game Plan for Life: Your Personal Playbook for Success*, is a wonderful book based on the views of the three times Super Bowl Champion and three time NASCAR Champion, Joe Gibbs. Although it is very much influenced by Joe's religious values, yet it might give guidance to anyone seeking to reach the pinnacle of the success ladder. Some of the points that are emphasized throughout state:

1. That if there is no game plan, one should not hope to obtain victory in any game or situation in life

2. That the world is trying to sell us a bill of goods, that is always significant for success.

3. That what is often perceived as success, sometimes leads to the trap of disaster

4. That in the game plan of life one needs to account for God.

5. That God is the Ultimate Coach, the Bible is the Ultimate Playbook,

6. That a true understanding of the teaching on creation will bring one to an authentic sense of identity,

7. That sin and addictions must be dealt with

8. That the central questions of life encircling salvation, relationships, finances, career, health, and heaven cannot be treated with disdain.

The point is when life is faced in the fullest way one is able to find one's true purpose and meaning. In fact, the recommendation is made that one is to assess one's life so that one with know when one is living in an unhealthy way.

Many other books could be recommended, however we have named only these three that have been the greatest influence during our writing. The common thread about them is that no one can succeed without purpose. Of course, what is liked about the latter is that it does not count success from a material perspective, but notes that one ought to take into account that the ultimate significance of success is what happens to a person at the end of life. On the bases of this final question we focused not only on Baseball but on Joseph, the great governor of Egypt.

IV   *The hidden influences behind how sports are played and games are won*, by Tobias J. Moskowitz & L. Jon Wertheim (2011), is profoundly exciting as an educational tool. By reflecting on the games that people play, it teaches many lessons about our life's maps. It is a profound piece of psychological work that uses the work of umpires, coaches, managers, and players to broaden our skills in decision making, risk taking and aggressiveness. You will do yourself a great favor if you will take the time to read it.

V.   *The Pact* and *The Bond* are two books that tell the story of three young men, Sampson Davis M. D., Rameck Hunt M. D., and George Jenkins DMD who beat just about every obstacle to become doctors. In one of the blurbs in the front leaf it is noted that "Each battled their own doubts and demons and managed to pull themselves out of dangerous situations through the strength of their friendship, to achieve success beyond their wildest dreams."

1.   They were born in Newark, in the projects, in broken homes.

2.   Their fathers offered little to no support.

3.   Their mothers were financially challenged, as many inner city single mothers are.

4.   But they made a pact to support other.

5.   And with the support of great teachers and mentors,

6.   They were able to beat the odds to become who they are today.

These two books are being recommended to many school districts across the USA. They are powerful personal reads.

In the book by Mark Victor Hanson, *The Richest Kids in America,* among other stories, tells the very inspiring story of Ephren Taylor. Here is a brief:

1.   Ephren is a black (now 28 years old) young man, born in Mississippi who rose from poverty to become the CEO of one of America's largest video corporation.

2.   When as a boy, Ephren wished to play video games, his mother who could not afford to pay for the games told him to go make up his own games.

3.   He taught himself how to program the computer and began to create his own video games and his idea began to grow until he formed a corporation.

4.   He is one of America big stock traders.

5.   He became so rich that his High School teacher left teaching to work for him.

6.   When asked what makes him so effective, he speaks of his great work ethic, how he turned his curiosity into creativity, and how he used his passion with purpose.

Other youngsters who are named in the book with Ephren state their conviction in the same way.

> T. Harve Eker's *Secrets of the Millionaire Mine: Mastering the Inner Game of Wealth* is a book that is also a rather interesting read, not so much because it encourages wealth, but because it tries to profile the minds of people who we often called successful.

Eker reminds his readers that what he is offering are principles for life's transformation.

Then he opens a blue print on why some persons are rich and why others are destined for a life of struggle.

He goes on to show how people are affected by what they believe (about money) and what they do not believe.

How people are impacted by their fear of failure or fear of success.

How commitment, focus, courage, determination, knowledge, and the use of opportunities function in regards to the rich and the poor.

Not everything about these books makes sense to us, but we consider them important to read.

We like to read them because:

Reading increases our knowledge

Reading expands our understanding of life

Reading makes us ready when we have to speak

Reading gives us enjoyment

Reading increases our literary skills

THEMES FOR CONTINUING INVESTIGATION

Leadership strategies for youth

Visioning strategies for youth

Confrontation strategies for youth

Money management strategies for youth

Anger management strategies for youth

Time management strategies for youth

Health management strategies for youth

Spiritual development strategies for youth

Social Media management strategies for youth

Getting equipped to achieve your dreams

Communication strategies for youth

Endurance strategies for youth

How to fix your mistakes

THINK OF YOUR LEGACY AS YOU DEVELOP YOUR LIFE MAP.

WHAT WOULD YOU LIKE TO LEAVE FOR THE GENERATIONS TO COME?

If you wish to receive information on how to obtain books, sponsor workshops or receive resources on any of the following areas:

Parental Legacy

Parental Advocacy

Life Maps Legacy

The Cyclical Nature of Relationships

The Legacy of Love

The Legacy of Faith

Contact: The Legacy Seminars

(862) 224-1265 (C)

Legacyseminars41@gmail.com

We have been working with family and youth legacy issues for more than 40 years now, and have found that the challenges facing families and youth are becoming more and more frustrating. Amidst the frustrations we find hope because we meet individuals who are willing to dialogue and set themselves on paths that are successful. We have seen many successes, but we consider them not enough, and thus our passion to bring a challenge one more time through **Life Maps Legacy.**

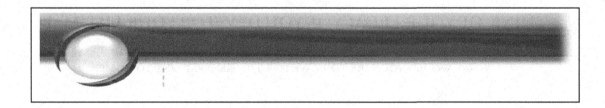